THE QUEEN'S KNIGHT

The Queen's Knight Vol. 8

Created by Kim Kang Won

Translation - Sora Han
English Adaptation - Kara Stambach
Retouch and Lettering - Star Print Brokers
Production Artist - Jennifer Carbajal
Graphic Designer - Monalisa De Asis

Editor - Troy Lewter
Digital Imaging Manager - Chris Buford
Pre-Production Supervisor - Erika Terriquez
Art Director - Anne Marie Horne
Production Manager - Elisabeth Brizzi
Managing Editor - Vy Nguyen
VP of Production - Ron Klamert
Editor-in-Chief - Rob Tokar
Publisher - Mike Kiley
President and C.O.O. - John Parker
C.E.O. and Chief Creative Officer - Stuart Levy

TOKYOPOP Inc.
5900 Wilshire Blvd. Suite 2000
Los Angeles, CA 90036

E-mail: info@TOKYOPOP.com
Come visit us online at www.TOKYOPOP.com

ISBN: 978-1-59532-264-7

First TOKYOPOP printing: February 2007

10 9 8 7 6 5 4 3 2 1

Printed in the USA

THE QUEEN'S KNIGHT

VOLUME 8

BY KIM KANG WON

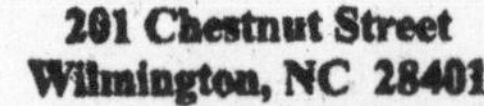

HAMBURG // LONDON // LOS ANGELES // TOKYO

LAST TIME IN...

THE QUEEN'S KNIGHT

YUNA IS A NORMAL GIRL WHO VISITS HER MOTHER IN GERMANY AND BEFALLS A TERRIBLE DISASTER. AFTER SHE RETURNS HOME FROM HER ACCIDENT, SHE BEGINS TO HAVE STRANGE DREAMS. IN HER DREAM, A KNIGHT WHO CALLS HIMSELF "RIENO" TELLS YUNA THAT SHE IS HIS QUEEN AND THAT HE IS HER KNIGHT. YUNA'S BROTHERS SEND HER BACK TO GERMANY, WHERE SHE MEETS THE KNIGHT FROM HER DREAMS--WHO THEN PROMPTLY KIDNAPS HER, TAKING HER TO PHANTASMA.

PHANTASMA IS A WORLD COVERED ENTIRELY WITH SNOW, AND YUNA IS FORCED TO LIVE WITH RIENO. BUT JUST WHEN YUNA WAS GETTING USED TO BEING WITH HIM, SPRING ARRIVES, AND YUNA IS TAKEN TO ELYSIAN TO BE PROPERLY INSTALLED AS THE QUEEN OF PHANTASMA. ONCE THERE, YUNA BEFRIENDS THE QUEEN'S GUARDIAN KNIGHTS, EHREN, LEON AND SCHILLER, THE HATEFUL CHANCELLOR KENT, AS WELL AS THE QUEEN'S RIVAL, PRINCESS LIBERA.

YUNA ALMOST IMMEDIATELY BEGINS TO SHAKE THINGS UP, AS SHE NOT ONLY REPEALS THE TAXES AND DECLARES SLAVERY ILLEGAL, BUT INSISTS ON PARTICIPATING IN THE FOREST OF DARKNESS HUNT, A DEADLY EXCURSION INTO THE DEMON-INFESTED FOREST. HOWEVER, LITTLE DOES SHE KNOW THAT LIBERA'S HIRED BANDITS PLAN TO AMBUSH YUNA AND HER HUNTING PARTY. BUT WHEN THEIR FIRST ARROW STRIKES YUNA'S PONY, THE FRIGHTENED ANIMAL GOES INTO A FRENZIED RUN THAT CARRIES YUNA DEEP WITHIN THE BOWELS OF THE DEMON-INFESTED FOREST.

ALL THE KNIGHTS SCRAMBLE TO SAVE YUNA, BUT IT IS EHREN THAT MANAGES TO MAKE IT TO HER IN TIME TO DEFEND HER FROM ZOMBIE WARRIORS. HOWEVER IT IS RIENO WHO RIDES IN AND SAVES THEM BOTH AT THE LAST MINUTE, LAYING WASTE ANY ZOMBIES IN HIS PATH. YUNA AND A SERIOUSLY INJURED EHREN ESCAPE ON REINO'S HORSE WHILE HE STAYS BEHIND TO FIGHT. YUNA PASSES OUT ALONG THE WAY... AND WAKES UP IN THE VILLAGE OF SCHWER. SHE LEARNS THAT THOUGH EHREN'S PHYSICAL WOUNDS ARE HEALING, HIS SOUL IS STILL IN PERIL. SCHILLER VOLUNTEERS TO TAKE HIM BACK TO THE FAIRY FOREST TO PERFORM A RITE TO BRING HIM BACK TO CONSCIOUSNESS. IT IS A DANGEROUS CEREMONY, BUT HE INSISTS ON TAKING THE RISK FOR EHREN. MEANWHILE, YUNA DEMANDS ANSWERS FROM HEMEL IN REGARDS TO HER OVERNIGHT HAIR GROWTH, AS WELL AS HER DESTINED RELATIONSHIP WITH RIENO. HE TELLS HER THAT IT CAN BE BECAUSE HER HEART IS FILLED WITH LOVE--BUT NOT NECESSARILY LOVE FOR RIENO.

WITH THIS REVELATION, THEY ALL CUT THE HUNT SHORT AND RETURN TO THE CASTLE, WHERE CHANCELLOR KENT IMMEDIATELY CHASTISES YUNA FOR ENDING THE HUNT EARLY. EVERYONE IS WONDERING IF YUNA IS INDEED IN LOVE...SO WHEN EHREN RETURNS, HE ADVISES YUNA TO PRETEND THAT HE IS THE OBJECT OF HER DESIRE, AT LEAST UNTIL SHE DISCOVERS THE REAL TRUTH. LATER, YUNA SHOWS EVERYONE HER BLUEPRINTS FOR THE HOSPITAL/SCHOOL, AND HERMENY TELLS HER OF THE DOOMED ROMANCE BETWEEN RIENO AND ELI, THE QUEEN BEFORE HER. LIBERA MAKES HER MOVE ON A RELUCTANT EHREN, AND YUNA CATCHES THEM MID-EMBRACE. LATER, WHILE LEON AND SCHILLER JEALOUSLY WATCH FROM THE SHADOWS, EHREN AND YUNA ALMOST KISS...BUT YUNA SUDDENLY TURNS AWAY AT THE LAST MINUTE, GIVING HER SUITORS RENEWED HOPE FOR WINNING HER HEART ONCE MORE.

Kang Won Kim
THE QUEEN'S KNIGHT

다각
다각

Intrigue

WE APOLOGIZE FOR YOUR LONG JOURNEY TO THE FOREST OF LIGHT, EHREN HWERUSUTE.
WELCOME.
I THOUGHT THIS WAS A PRIVATE MEETING...
THE FAIRY KING, RULER OF THIS FOREST, HAS COME TO GREET US.
NOW WE SHALL BE ON OUR WAY.
NO ONE CAN EAVESDROP ON YOUR CONVERSATION, NOR CAN ANYONE INTERFERE...YOU CAN REST EASY AND SPEAK IN PRIVATE HERE.

HEMEL! ARE YOU ONE OF THE FAIRIES?
HA HA HA...! NO, I AM NOT KIN TO THE FAIRIES... SCHILLER IS NOT A FAIRY EITHER.
BUT, I SUPPOSE YOU CAN'T DENY THAT HE DOES HAVE SOME FAIRY BLOOD IN HIM...

FOR COUNTLESS AGES, WE'VE BEEN LIVING WITH THE LIGHT CLAN. YOU COULD SAY THAT WE'VE BEEN INFLUENCED QUITE A BIT BY THEM...
FAIRIES OF THE LIGHT CLAN CANNOT RAISE THEIR CHILDREN, NOT EVEN AFTER GIVING BIRTH TO THEM.
SINCE ANCIENT TIMES, THEY'VE LEFT THEIR CHILDREN IN MY VILLAGE...
FOR THAT REASON, THE FAIRY CHILDREN AND THE VILLAGE CHILDREN ALL GREW UP TOGETHER.

HERE--WINE MADE BY THE FAIRIES THEMSELVES.
......
HONESTLY...
THAT'S WHY WE'RE A LOT CLOSER TO THE LIGHT CLAN THAN MOST.
IN ADDITION, THERE ARE A FEW INSTANCES OF MIXING BLOOD...

HEMEL--BEFORE COMING HERE, I RESEARCHED THE HISTORY OF PHANTASMA AND RIENO'S BACKGROUND.
BUT NO MATTER HOW HARD I SOUGHT, I COULDN'T FIND ANY INFORMATION ON THE PAST LORD OF THE DUNKKAR MANOR, REINHART RIENO GROSS...
...OR THE PRESENT LORD, **RIENO.**
IF RIENO IS HUMAN, AND NOT A PART OF THE LIGHT CLAN-- HOW DOES HE AVOID BEING INFLUENCED BY PHANTASMA'S TIME OR AGE...
...LIKE YOU OR THE OTHER LIGHT CLAN MEMBERS?

IS THIS ALL POSSIBLE BECAUSE OF THE PAST QUEENS' **CURSE?**

MY FATHER PASSED AWAY TOO SUDDENLY... WITHOUT TELLING ME ANYTHING AT ALL.
IF WHAT I'VE JUST TOLD YOU IS SOMEHOW CONNECTED WITH YOU CALLING ME HERE...
...THEN I MUST KNOW! HEMEL, THERE ARE SO MANY TRUTHS THAT LIE HIDDEN BENEATH WHAT'S ACTUALLY REVEALED TO THE WORLD...

EHREN HWERUSUTE...
...CAN YOU TELL ME WITHOUT ANY DOUBT IN YOUR MIND THAT THE QUEEN'S GROWTH WAS DUE TO YOU?
!
OF COURSE.

THEN, WHAT ABOUT YOU?
ARE YOU WILLING TO DO ANYTHING FOR THE SAKE OF THE QUEEN...NOT AS ONE LOYAL TO THE CROWN, BUT AS A MAN WHO LOVES HER?
......
LET'S JUST SAY...
...CAN YOU PERSUADE THE QUEEN TO PLUNGE A DAGGER INTO RIENO'S HEART?

IN ADDITION...

...HAVE YOU COME TO ME TODAY AS A MAN WHO DESIRES NOTHING BUT TO PROTECT THE WOMAN HE LOVES?
OR HAVE YOU COME TO ME AS THE HEAD OF YOUR FAMILY AND FUTURE CHANCELLOR...
...WHO WANTS ONLY TO SAVE PHANTASMA FROM ITS DESTINY?
BA-THUMP!
BA-THUMP!
BA-THUMP!
SO WHICH IS IT? MY ANSWER DEPENDS ON YOUR RESPONSE, EHREN HWERUSUTE!!

Yuna's handmade attire.

IT'S GOOD. EVEN THOUGH YOU MAY NOT UNDERSTAND RIGHT NOW, YOU'LL SEE SOON ENOUGH!
WE'RE JUST GONNA TRY THIS, WHATEVER THE OUTCOME!
SCHOOLS...
HOSPITALS...
PLAY-GROUNDS...

YOUR MAJESTY!
WHO THREW THAT?!
LET'S GET OUTTA HERE!!

STOP WHERE YOU ARE, YOU LITTLE TWERPS!!
ARE YOU ALL RIGHT, YOUR HIGHNESS?
웅성
웅성
웅성
UH-HUH...
웅성
IF WE COULD JUST BORROW SOMEONE'S HOUSE FOR A MOMENT...
JUST TO WASH HER OFF...EVEN A LITTLE BIT...!
웅성 ....
웅성 ...
AHEM...

HMPH! I HEAR THE QUEEN'S IN LOVE WITH RIENO...!
HOW CAN SHE BE SHAMELESS ENOUGH TO WALK AROUND IN BROAD DAYLIGHT?!
QUEEN? WHAT QUEEN? SHE'S JUST A KITTY IN HEAT...!
HOW COME THE GHOSTS DON'T SPIRIT RIENO AWAY?
I'M SO TIRED! I'M SICK OF LIVING LIKE THIS!

SO IS THAT THE RUMOR THAT'S GOING AROUND?
THAT THE QUEEN'S GROWTH WAS PROMPTED BY RIENO...?
HEH...! THIS IS INTERESTING...
SO, THE RUMOR IS SNOWBALLING, GETTING BIGGER AND BIGGER...
...AND IT'S BECOMING THE GENERAL OPINION OF ALL THE PEOPLE.
SO DID THAT GIRL RUN BACK TO THE PALACE IN TEARS?
NO, SHE DID NOT. SHE WALKED BACK PROUDLY, COVERED IN DIRTY WATER.
RIGHT NOW, CHANCELLOR KENT IS IN AN EXECUTIVE COUNCIL MEETING.

WHY ISN'T EHREN ON THE ROSTER TO RECEIVE A TITLE OF NOBILITY?

WHAT TITLE? HE DESERTED IN THE MIDDLE OF THE HUNT!

I UNDERSTAND THAT YOU FAVOR EHREN--BUT HOW CAN YOU INTERFERE IN THESE AFFAIRS?

DON'T EVEN **SAY THAT!** EHREN FOUGHT SO DILIGENTLY THAT HE ALMOST PAID WITH HIS **LIFE!!**

BESIDES, HE'S YOUR OWN NEPHEW...! SAYING HE RAN AWAY IS A BIT HARSH, DON'T YOU THINK?!
YUNA SEEMS A TAD HYSTERICAL.
JUST WHAT IS THIS?!
UH-HUH...I THINK THE INCIDENT IN THE VILLAGE SHOCKED HER...
WHY DO YOU KEEP GOING AGAINST MY COMMANDS TO BUILD A SCHOOL AND A HOSPITAL IN THIS COUNTRY?!
IF SHE'S QUEEN, SHE SHOULD JUST SIT QUIETLY IN THE PALACE, LOOKING PRETTY! WHY IS SHE INTERFERING?!
NO WONDER ALL THE PEOPLE ARE AGAINST HER...
WHAT DID YOU SAY...?!
WHAT?!
AGAIN?

IT LOOKS LIKE A DAUGHTER REBELLING AGAINST HER FATHER.
IN ANY CASE, SHE'S REALLY SOMETHING.
I WILL DEFINITELY SUCCEED IN BUILDING A SCHOOL AND HOSPITAL! EAT THAT!
THAT'S YUNA'S APPEAL...
AMAZING...

HM...YOU ARE EHREN HWERUSUTE TO THE BONE...! YOU TRULY ARE THE CHANCELLOR'S SUCCESSOR.
IN PHANTASMA'S PRESENT SITUATION...
...HOW MANY THINGS CAN WE SOLVE WITH LOVE ALONE?
DO NOT UNDERESTIMATE THE POWER OF LOVE, EHREN.
HAVE YOU FORGOTTEN THAT LOVE IS THE VERY THING THAT BRINGS SPRING TO PHANTASMA?

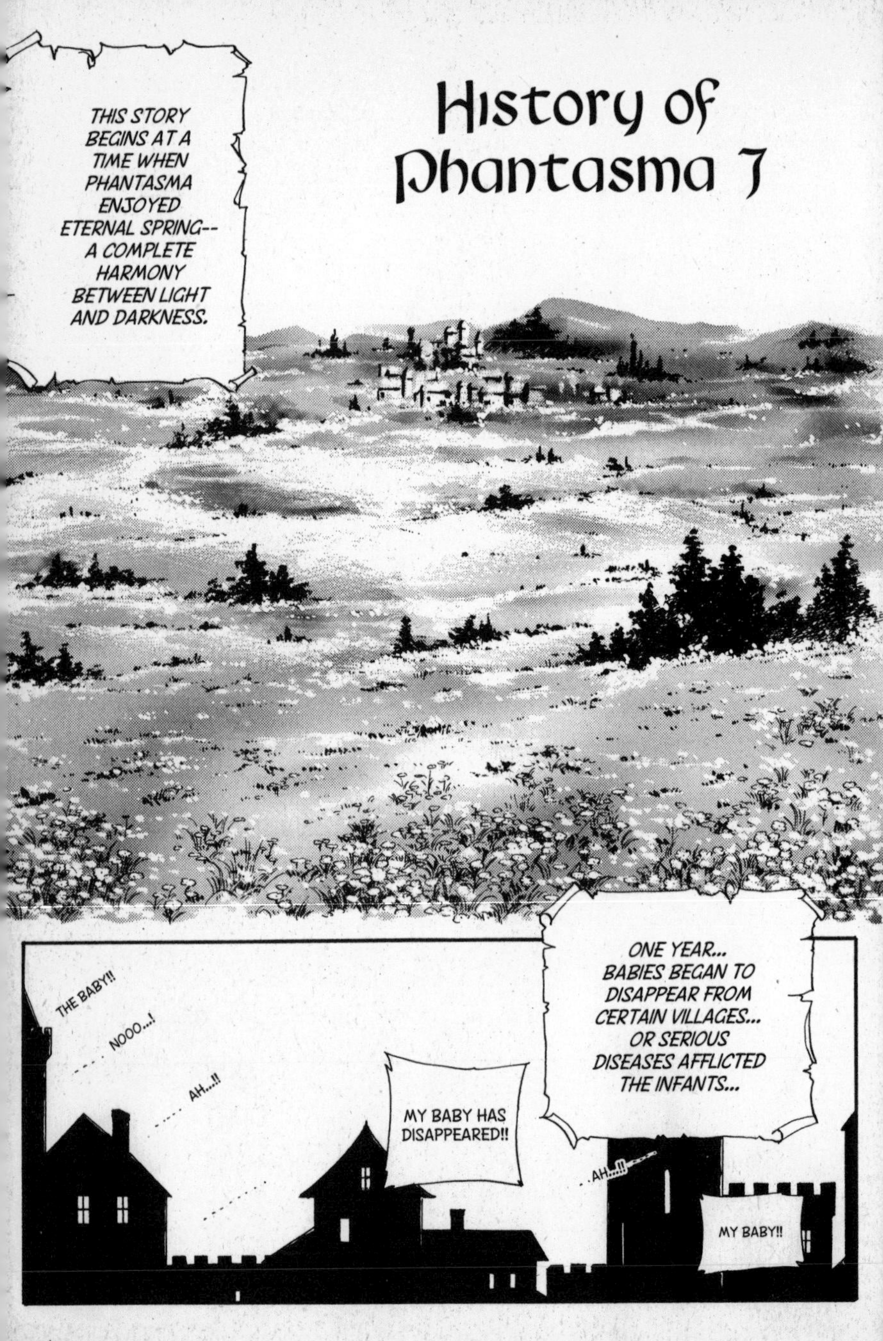
History of Phantasma 7
THIS STORY BEGINS AT A TIME WHEN PHANTASMA ENJOYED ETERNAL SPRING-- A COMPLETE HARMONY BETWEEN LIGHT AND DARKNESS.
ONE YEAR... BABIES BEGAN TO DISAPPEAR FROM CERTAIN VILLAGES... OR SERIOUS DISEASES AFFLICTED THE INFANTS...
MY BABY HAS DISAPPEARED!!
THE BABY!!
NOOO...!
AH...!!
..AH...!!
MY BABY!!

ALL SORTS OF HORRIBLE THINGS WERE HAPPENING TO THE CHILDREN.
THE QUEEN EVEN ISSUED A COMMAND TO INVESTIGATE THE REASON BEHIND THE HORRORS...
MUCH LATER, IT WAS REALIZED THAT THE CAUSE...
...WAS HEXE, THE WITCH OF THE DARK ARTS, USING HER BLACK MAGIC.

HEXE WAS BORN IN AN OBSCURE VILLAGE NEAR THE FOREST OF DARKNESS...
SHE WAS KNOWN FOR HER BEAUTY AND PRACTICAL INGENUITY.
THAT SAID, SHE FELL IN LOVE WITH A YOUNG MAN, AND EVEN BORE HIS CHILD.
HOWEVER, WHEN HE DISCOVERED SHE WAS A WITCH OF THE DARK ARTS, THE YOUNG MAN TRIED TO KILL HER WHILE SHE WAS PREGNANT.
BUT HEXE DID NOT DIE. SHE WAS ABLE TO CLING TO LIFE... BUT IN THE PROCESS, SHE LOST THE CHILD IN HER WOMB.
FROM THAT POINT ON--SHE PLOTTED HER REVENGE.

SHE TOOK HER ANGER OUT ON NEWBORN BABIES AND LITTLE CHILDREN, SPREADING MALADIES AND CAUSING ALL SORTS OF ATROCITIES...

...WITH NO REGARD FOR WHETHER THEY WERE HUMANS, FAIRIES, OR BEASTS.

THE FAIRIES DECIDED THAT THEY COULD NO LONGER SIT IDLY BY, AND THEY MADE PLANS TO CAPTURE HEXE... BUT SHE WENT INTO HIDING.

THE WORLD QUIETED AND PEACE WAS ONCE AGAIN RESTORED.

쿵

쿵쿵

쿵 쿵

쿵

AT LEAST, THAT'S WHAT WAS BELIEVED...

WHAT'S GOING ON?
SIRE... TH-THERE'S A WOMAN HERE.
Reinhart Rieno Gross, Lord of the village of Dunkkar in Northern Phantasma.
IS SHE DEAD?
SHE'S STILL ALIVE!

크두두두 —— ...
크두두두
LORD REINHART IS BACK!!
WHAT BRINGS YOU HERE? SHOULDN'T YOU BE ATTENDING THE QUEEN?
히이이이...
HA HA HA! IT'S BEEN A WHILE, REINHART. I SEE YOU STILL ENJOY HUNTING.
AND PHANTASMA'S GREATEST HORSE, PAPHNER, IS LOOKING FINE AS ALWAYS!! IT REALLY IS...WORTHY OF EVERYONE'S ENVY...

DURING THE UPCOMING THANKSGIVING FESTIVAL...
...THE QUEEN WILL BE MAKING AN IMPORTANT DECISION BEFORE ALL THE LORDS AND NOBLES.
OUR BEAUTIFUL AND YOUNG QUEEN...
...HAS ALWAYS TAKEN A KEEN INTEREST IN YOU. YOU KNEW THIS, DIDN'T YOU, REINHART?
PERHAPS SHE HAS BEEN WATCHING YOU WIN TOURNAMENT AFTER TOURNAMENT. SHE SEEMS TO HAVE SPECIAL FEELINGS FOR YOU...HEH HEH HEH...!

IT'S DEFINITELY TIME THE QUEEN GETS A...*AHEM*... HUSBAND.
IS EHREN HWERUSUTE'S SON, KENT, AS LOUD AS EVER?
HA HA HA! IT'S JUST SO IRONIC THAT A DISMAL AND FAINT-HEARTED MAN LIKE KENT IS A PART OF THAT GREAT FAMILY LINE...!
I'LL SAY...! TO THINK THAT KENT ACTUALLY WANTS TO COMPETE IN THE UPCOMING TOURNAMENT! HA HA HA!

MY LORD...!
EVERYONE--
LEAVE MY
PRESENCE.

AH!
YOU...? I WILL TAKE YOU TO ELYSIAN BEFORE THE QUEEN.
ONLY THE QUEEN CAN PERMIT THE MARRIAGE OF A LORD...

WHO YOU ARE AND WHERE YOU'RE FROM...
...IS NOT IMPORTANT TO ME.
IF YOU DON'T WANT TO TELL ME ANYTHING, I WON'T EVEN ASK.
I WANT YOU TO HAVE MY CHILD--A STRONG, MIGHTY SON.

번쩍
THE SUCCESSOR OF DUNKKAR VILLAGE...

UGH...
MY BABY... G-GIVE ME BACK MY B-BABY...
I WON'T FORGIVE YOU...
GIVE ME BACK MY BABY!
MY BABY... GIVE ME BACK... MY BABY!

YOU WANT TO GIVE BIRTH TO A MONSTER?!
YOU MUST DIE!! YOU MONSTER!!
AHHHHHH!!
YOU THINK I'M JUST GOING TO LET YOU HAVE THE BABY?
YOU HID THE FACT THAT YOU'RE A WITCH JUST SO YOU COULD HAVE A BABY...!!
I'M GOING TO KILL YOU...
...AND EVERYONE ELSE!
STOP...
STOP IT NOW...!
I CAN NEVER HAVE CHILDREN AGAIN...
I CAN NEVER GIVE BIRTH TO A CHILD EVER AGAIN...!

DARK ENERGY HAS SEEPED INTO EVERY PART OF YOUR BODY FROM OVERUSING THE DARK ARTS...

...SO YOU MAY NEVER BE ABLE TO HAVE A CHILD... AND EVEN IF YOU DO, IT'LL MOST LIKELY BE A MONSTER OR A DARK CREATURE.

WHO'S THERE?!
OH YE ENGULFED BY THE DARKNESS...
...YOUR COMPLAINTS AND FURY HAVE STIRRED ALL OF HADES...YOUR RAGE HAS DRAWN ME HERE.
I WILL GIVE YOU A CHILD...
...IF YOU SO DESIRE...

WH- WHAT...?
THAT IS... IF YOU PROMISE ME ONE THING...
NO...
NO! NOT A MONSTER!
I'LL HAVE A MONSTER OR A STRANGE CREATURE!
I DON'T WANT TO GIVE BIRTH TO A BEAST!
DON'T WORRY... YOU'LL HAVE A HANDSOME, HEALTHY BABY BOY...

......
THAT'S RIGHT...IF YOU PROMISE ME...
A... BABY BOY?
A HEALTHY... NORMAL...
PROMISE?
WHAT KIND...
...OF PROMISE...?

YOU MUST SEND YOUR SON TO ME WHEN HE REACHES THE AGE OF NINETEEN!

GASP!
HUFF!
HUFF!
HUFF!
HUFF!
HUFF!
HUFF!
HUFF!

WE'RE ALMOST AT THE PALACE, SIRE.
다각
다각
WAIT...!
다각 다각 ......
쿠두두 둥...
다각
다각 ...

Queen Freyja
of Phantasma
OH, MY...
SIR REINHART!
WHAT A COINCIDENCE
MEETING YOU
HERE...!
IT'S BEEN
A LONG
TIME, YOUR
HIGHNESS.

I'VE REALLY MISSED YOU. OTHER PEOPLE VISIT THE PALACE FREQUENTLY...
...BUT YOU ONLY STOP BY DURING THANKSGIVING. YOU'RE HORRIBLE...!
......
....
빠으빠라라라...

NEXT...
SIR REINHART
RIENO GROSS OF
DUNKKAR VILLAGE.
BILT, LORD
OF NIDRIHEI
VILLAGE.
I'M SO JEALOUS...
DOES THAT MEAN
THAT THE LORD OF
DUNKKAR VILLAGE
WILL BECOME
THE QUEEN'S
HUSBAND?
DID YOU HEAR?
THE QUEEN
ALREADY SENT
HER ATTENDANT
TO EXPRESS
HER WISHES.
저벅
YOUNG QUEEN
FREYJA SEEMS
TO HAVE FINALLY
CHOSEN HER
HUSBAND.
저벅

I AM VERY EXCITED TO SEE YOUR PARTICIPATION IN THE TOURNAMENT. WHO WILL BE THE ONE TO RECEIVE YOUR CROWN OF VICTORY?
I WILL DO MY BEST TO FULFILL YOUR EXPECTATIONS.
MAY YOU ALSO BE KIND ENOUGH TO GIVE ME YOUR BLESSING FOR MY MARRIAGE?
MA- MARRIAGE...?
술렁
술렁

I INTRODUCE TO YOU ALL THE FUTURE MISTRESS OF DUNKKAR VILLAGE...

THAT DAY... WHEN HEXE FIRST APPEARED VIA THE INTRODUCTION OF THE LORD OF DUNKKAR VILLAGE, REINHART RIENO GROSS...
...THE FAIRIES, HEMEL, THE QUEEN...NO ONE KNEW HER TRUE IDENTITY.
웅성
웅성

THE FOUR-DAY THANKSGIVING TOURNAMENT BEGAN...
와
와
...AND JUST AS EXPECTED, REINHART RIENO GROSS WON THE TOURNAMENT, AND THE VICTOR'S CROWN WENT TO HIS BEAUTIFUL FIANCÉE...
와
와
THAT YEAR, ALTHOUGH THE PARTY COMMEMORATING THE TOURNAMENT WAS EXTRAVAGANT... THE COLD, TENSE ATMOSPHERE COULD NOT BE IGNORED.

WHAT DO YOU MEAN?! YOU STILL HAVEN'T DISCOVERED ANYTHING ABOUT THAT WOMAN?
HOW DOES THAT MAKE ANY SENSE? YOU DON'T EVEN KNOW WHO SHE IS OR WHERE SHE'S FROM?!
QUEEN FREYJA CONTINUED TO DELAY GIVING HER PERMISSION FOR THE LORD OF DUNKKAR TO GET MARRIED.
IS THAT SO?
EVERYONE HAD AN IDEA AS TO HER REASONS, BUT NO ONE DARED SAY IT OUT LOUD.
......

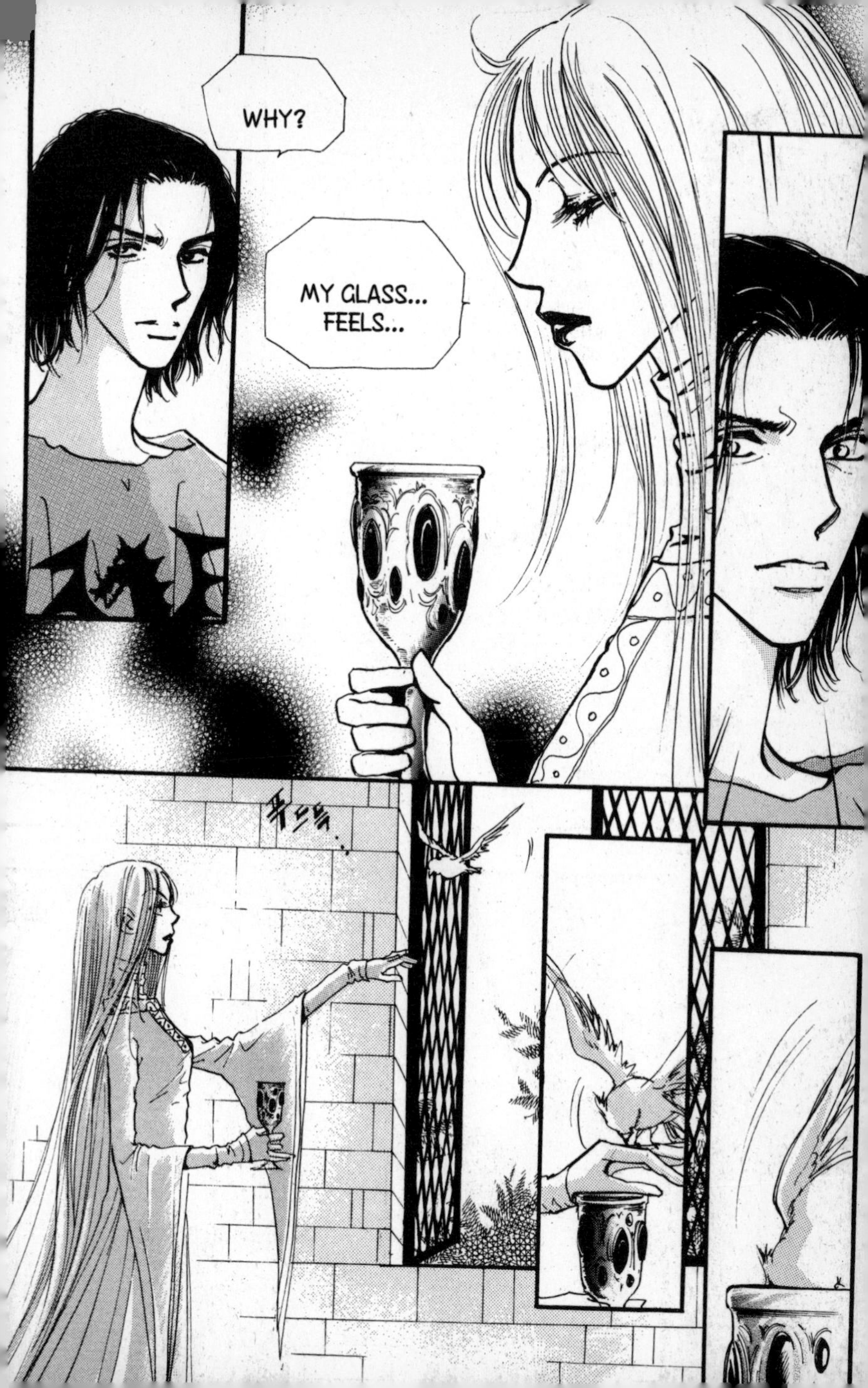
WHY?
MY GLASS... FEELS...
푸드득...

푸득
푸득
푸득
툭
HA HA HA!
하하하
YOUR HIGHNESS...
HA HA HA!

PLEASE PERMIT ME TO LEAVE THE PALACE TOMORROW.
MY FIANCÉE IS PREGNANT AND I WOULD LIKE TO RETURN TO MY VILLAGE BEFORE TRAVELING IS TOO DIFFICULT FOR HER.
D-DID YOU JUST SAY... PREGNANT? THAT WOMAN?
YES, YOUR HIGHNESS...SO PLEASE GIVE ME YOUR PERMISSION TO MARRY HER.

REINHART!
REINHART!
ONE MOMENT...!
PLEASE, I BEG OF YOU-- DON'T LEAVE! PLEASE...!!
I MEAN... WHAT ABOUT ME...?

I'M ALWAYS THINKING ABOUT YOU...ALWAYS...
IN ALL THE PAST THANKSGIVING CELEBRATIONS, I'VE SEARCHED FOR YOU ONLY...
YOU'RE THE ONLY ONE... WHOM I WANT TO TAKE AS MY HUSBAND...
I WANTED TO MATURE QUICKLY...
...BECAUSE I WANTED TO BECOME A WOMAN FIT FOR YOU...SO I COULD RECEIVE YOUR LOVE.
I FINALLY THOUGHT THAT THE TIME HAD NEARED...
YOUR HIGHNESS... I...

...I'M NOT A
STALLION TO SIMPLY
CHOOSE FROM
YOUR STABLE.

YOU--!!
쫘악!

I WILL NEVER... NEVER... PERMIT IT!

I WILL NEVER PERMIT THE CHILD IN THAT WOMAN'S WOMB TO HAVE YOUR NAME OR YOUR LAND!

후다닥

......

IT'S...VERY STRANGE...
THESE DAYS, I FREQUENTLY GET AN OMINOUS FEELING WHEN I'M IN THE PALACE.
RIGHT NOW, I JUST FELT A POWERFUL SURGE OF DARK ENERGY.
NOW THAT I THINK ABOUT IT, THERE WAS A PROPHECY MADE BY A SAGE WHO LIVES NEAR THE FAIRY FOREST.
THAT AFTER TEN FULL MOONS... A CURSE WILL BEFALL US ALL...

I RECENTLY READ THE SAME SIGNS IN THE STARS...
YOU TOO, HEMEL?
THE REASON WHY PHANTASMA WAS ABLE TO ENJOY ETERNAL SPRING...
...WAS BECAUSE OF THE STRENGTH OF THE QUEENS, WHO ARE THE SUCCESSORS OF THE PEOPLE OF LIGHT.
BECAUSE OF THEM, THE LIGHT CONTINUED TO FLOURISH IN STRENGTH, DRIVING THE DARKNESS OUT...
THE PRESSURE WAS SO INTENSE, HOWEVER... THINGS WERE ON THE VERGE OF EXPLODING.

PHANTASMA IS A WORLD THAT EXISTS THROUGH THE BALANCE OF LIGHT AND DARKNESS.
WE WERE WORRIED BECAUSE THERE WERE OMINOUS SIGNS THAT FORETOLD SOME DREADFUL EVENT IN THE NEAR FUTURE.
HOW CAN THIS BE...?
WHAT'S THE MATTER, ELDER?
HOW CAN THIS HAPPEN...?

MY GOODNESS...
THE FORCES OF DARKNESS...THE SUCCESSOR TO THE THRONE OF DARKNESS HAS BEEN CONCEIVED.
H-HOW COULD THIS...?
AH...BUT I CAN'T SEE CLEARLY ENOUGH. IT'S BEING SHIELDED BY ANOTHER FORCE.
A GREAT SHIELD OF STRENGTH IS OBSTRUCTING A CLEAR VISION...

YOUR HIGHNESS-- PLEASE GRANT SIR REINHART PERMISSION TO MARRY.
SHUT UP...!! I WILL NEVER DO THAT!!
THIS IS FOR YOUR SAKE, YOUR HIGHNESS. AT THIS TIME, ALL THE NOBLES ARE WATCHING YOUR EVERY MOVEMENT.
YOUR CURRENT EMOTIONAL STATE WILL NOT PROVE BENEFICIAL TO YOU IN ANY WAY.
PLEASE SHOW US A MORE MATURE APPEARANCE.
I WILL TAKE CARE OF THE REST.
PLEASE TRUST ME. I, EHREN HWERUSUTE, CAN BE TRUSTED... PLEASE...

AH...
AH...
THE QUEEN GRANTED PERMISSION FOR THE LORD OF DUNKKAR VILLAGE TO GET MARRIED...
AS REINHART RIENO GROSS WAS RETURNING TO HIS VILLAGE, SHE SENT ASSASSINS FIVE TIMES TO HINDER HIM...
허이이잉
REGARDLESS, HE ARRIVED SAFELY AT DUNKKAR.
AND...

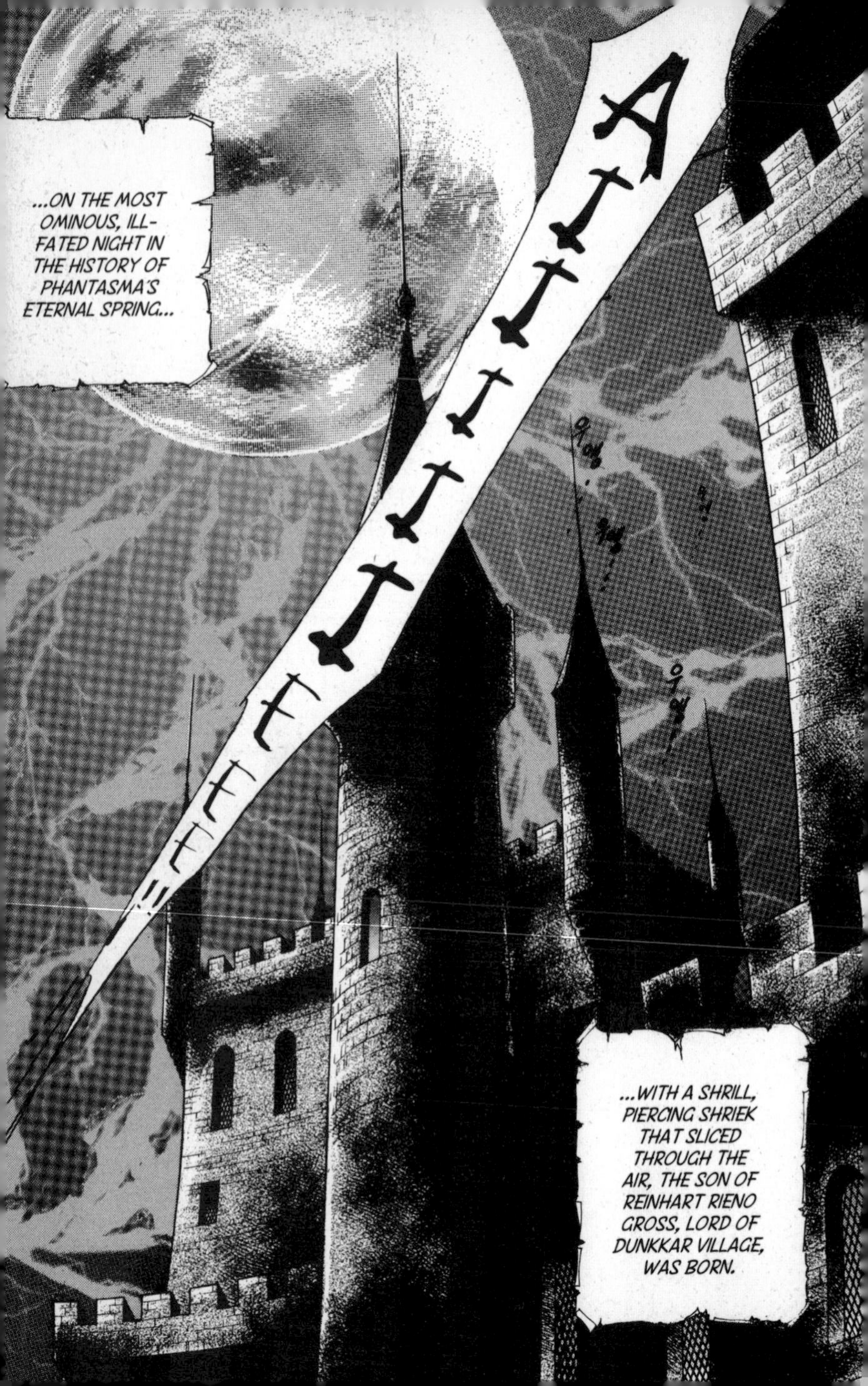
...ON THE MOST OMINOUS, ILL-FATED NIGHT IN THE HISTORY OF PHANTASMA'S ETERNAL SPRING...
AIIIIIEEEE!!
...WITH A SHRILL, PIERCING SHRIEK THAT SLICED THROUGH THE AIR, THE SON OF REINHART RIENO GROSS, LORD OF DUNKKAR VILLAGE, WAS BORN.

A HANDSOME, HEALTHY BABY BOY...

DO NOT FORGET THE PROMISE YOU HAVE MADE ME...

WHEN HE REACHES THE AGE OF NINETEEN, HIS SOUL WILL BELONG TO ME...

UNTIL THEN, LOVE HIM AND CARE FOR HIM ALL YOU WANT.

I AM EAGER TO SEE WHAT TYPE OF MAN THE SON OF A WITCH WHOSE BLOOD IS TAINTED WITH DARK MAGIC WILL BE...

NEVER...
I WILL NEVER HAND OVER MY SON!!
I WILL NOT SIT STILL AND BE CONTROLLED BY THE DARK POWERS.
I WILL PROTECT YOU WITH EVERYTHING I HAVE, EVEN IF IT TAKES EVERY LAST DROP OF BLOOD IN MY BODY...
MY BABY... I WILL NEVER... NEVER... HAND YOU OVER...!

WHETHER IT'S THE DEMON KING OF DARKNESS...OR AN ABSOLUTE POWER IN THIS WORLD...
...I WILL GIVE EVERYTHING I HAVE TO PROTECT YOU!!

JUST IMPOSING A TAX IS TOO WEAK.
THE CITIZENS OF HIS VILLAGE ARE ALREADY LEAVING BECAUSE THE TAX IS TOO MUCH FOR THEM.
HOWEVER, RIENO GROSS IS JUST AS SILENT AS EVER. HE SIMPLY BEARS THE NEW BURDENS.
I'M GOING TO MAKE HIM SUFFER, JUST AS MUCH AS I'M SUFFERING RIGHT NOW...!
I'LL SUFFOCATE HIM!

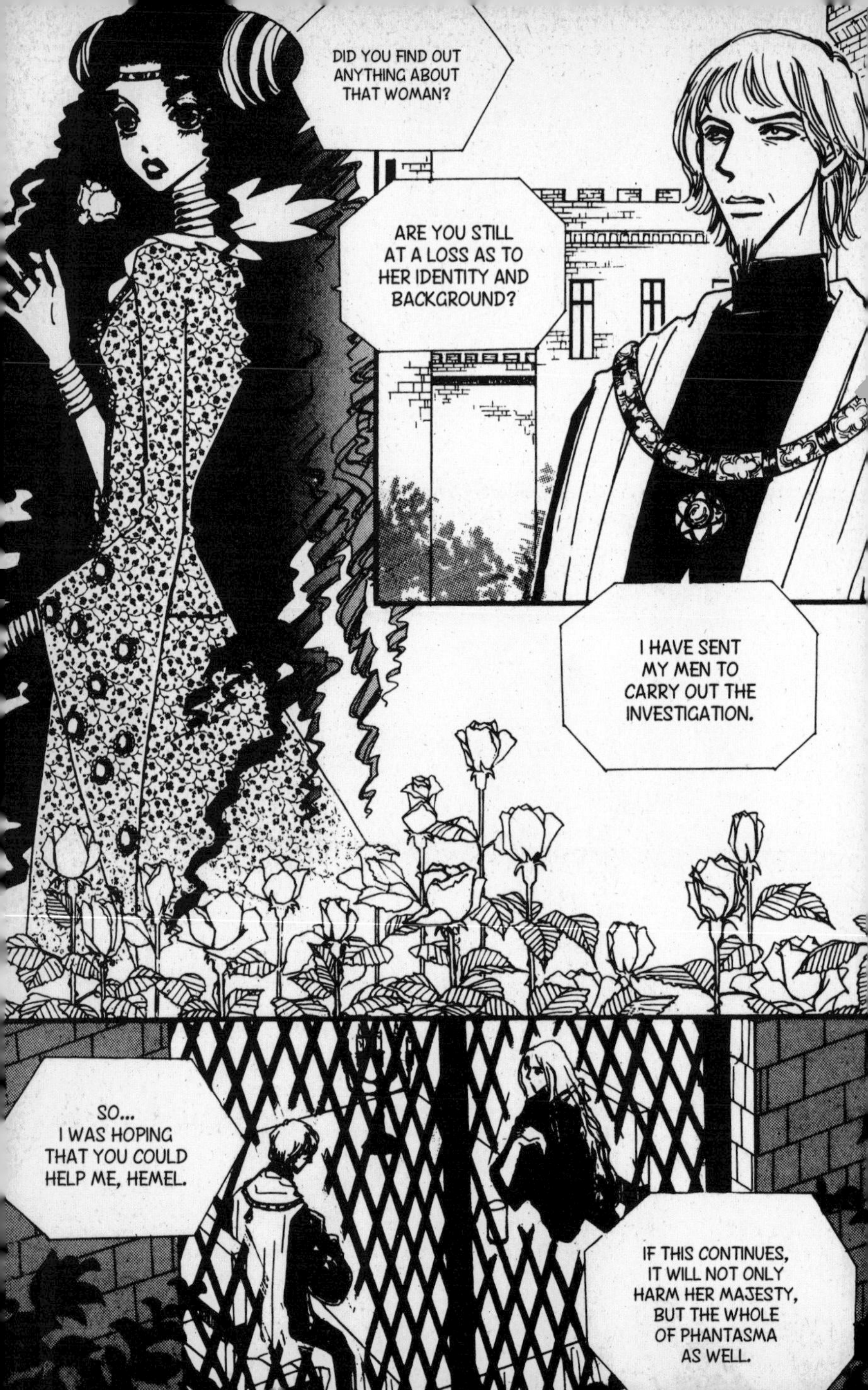
DID YOU FIND OUT ANYTHING ABOUT THAT WOMAN?
ARE YOU STILL AT A LOSS AS TO HER IDENTITY AND BACKGROUND?
I HAVE SENT MY MEN TO CARRY OUT THE INVESTIGATION.
SO... I WAS HOPING THAT YOU COULD HELP ME, HEMEL.
IF THIS CONTINUES, IT WILL NOT ONLY HARM HER MAJESTY, BUT THE WHOLE OF PHANTASMA AS WELL.

WE MUST QUICKLY RESOLVE THIS ISSUE WITH RIENO GROSS AND HELP THE QUEEN MOVE ON.
I WANT PHANTASMA TO RETURN TO ITS ORIGINAL STATE--AN ABUNDANT AND TRANQUIL LAND.
WHAT DO YOU WANT ME TO DO?
RIENO GROSS...HIS WIFE, HIS SON, HIS ENTIRE FAMILY--I WANT YOU TO KILL THEM ALL.
THIS INCIDENT WILL CONSUME SIGNIFICANT TIME, AND THE CONSEQUENCES WILL IMPACT US GREATLY. THAT IS, IF YOU AGREE TO HELP ME...

IT SOUNDS AS IF YOU WANT ME TO DEVISE AN UNDERHANDED PLOT...
...AND USE MY POWERS TO HARM OTHERS.

IT'S UNREASONABLE FOR YOU TO ASK ME TO DO SUCH A THING...

...SIMPLY BECAUSE HER MAJESTY IS NOT HAPPY ABOUT WHAT HAS HAPPENED.

IF YOU HAD A MORE VALID REASON, THEN MAYBE...

I'M...SO DIZZY...
I'VE ALREADY BEEN ON EDGE...
저벅
저벅
A FEW MONTHS AGO, AFTER THE APPEARANCE OF AN OMINOUS STAR IN THE NORTH...
저벅
...I WAS ALREADY ON EDGE THINKING ABOUT THAT.

WHO'S THERE? REVEAL YOURSELF!

.....

BUT--

I **SAID** YOU MAY **RETURN.** NOW STOP BOTHERING ME!

YES...
WHERE IN THE WORLD IS SHE SNEAKING OFF TO? SHE DOESN'T EVEN HAVE HER MAIDS WITH HER...AND SHE'S CARRYING HER BABY, TOO...
......
I WONDER IF I'M SUPPOSED TO REPORT THINGS LIKE THIS TO THE PALACE...
A HUT...?

GASP!

A...
WITCH!
GASP!
HUFF!
A
WITCH!!
ACK...!!
THE
MISTRESS OF
THE HOUSE
IS A WITCH!!

SO WHAT?
MANY PEOPLE HAVE ALREADY LEFT THE VILLAGE BECAUSE OF THE EXORBITANT TAX IMPOSED UPON OUR CITIZENS BY THE PALACE. THE NUMBER OF PEOPLE FLEEING BY NIGHT IS EVER INCREASING.
IF YOU DON'T PUT ADEQUATE MEASURES IN PLACE...WE'LL BE IN DIRE STRAIGHTS.

MEASURES?
SOMEONE FROM THE PALACE ALERTED ME TO THE FACT THAT...
...ALL OF THIS IS HAPPENING BECAUSE OF THE MISTRESS.
......
AND...THESE DAYS THERE'S A RUMOR... THAT THE MISTRESS IS A BIT STRANGE, AND, WELL...THAT SHE MAY NOT BE HUMAN.

WOULD YOU KINDLY REPEAT THAT?

I-I'M... I'M JUST T-TELLING YOU THE RUMORS THAT ARE SPREADING RIGHT NOW...

IF YOU SAY ANYTHING GROUNDLESS ABOUT MY WIFE AND SON AGAIN, I'LL RIP YOUR THROAT OUT.

RIENO GROSS! WHAT ARE YOU HESITATING FOR? LEAVE THAT WOMAN! ALL YOU NEED TO DO IS LEAVE HER!
THE QUEEN IS TAKING REVENGE BECAUSE OF HER FEELINGS TOWARD YOU! WHAT WILL YOU DO? WILL YOU JUST SINK LIKE THIS?
SIRE...

SIRE...I DON'T KNOW HOW I SH-SHOULD TELL YOU THIS...

WHAT'S WRONG?

REALLY! I SAW IT OUT THERE WITH MY VERY OWN EYES!
IF SHE WASN'T A WITCH, WHY WOULD SHE DO SUCH QUEER THINGS?!
WHAT DO YOU MEAN, "OUT THERE"?!
IT'S...THIS PARTICULAR PLACE.
TO BE HONEST...I'VE BEEN FOLLOWING THE MISTRESS FOR A WHILE.
WHAT IS ALL THIS?!
EVERY DAY SHE SNEAKS OUT OF THE PALACE AND COMES TO THIS PLACE...

WHO TOLD YOU TO FOLLOW THE MISTRESS?
SIRE?
....
덜 덜
I'VE COMMITTED A GRAVE SIN, SIRE!
A WHILE AGO, A PALACE OFFICIAL CAME AND ASKED ME TO FOLLOW THE MISTRESS AND REPORT ON HER EVERY MOVEMENT...!
SO... DID YOU TELL THIS TO ANYONE ELSE?
N-NO...! AS SOON AS I FOUND OUT, I CAME TO YO--

WAAAHHH...
WAAAHHH...

MISTRESS, THE YOUNG MASTER KEEPS CRYING! WHAT SHOULD I--
IT'S ALL RIGHT. YOU MAY LEAVE. THE BABY IS JUST A LITTLE TIRED.

I-I'LL TAKE MY LEAVE, MILADY.
DARLING...

SOME FOOL SAID THAT MY SON IS THE SPAWN OF A WITCH.

THAT WOULD MEAN MY WIFE, THE MOTHER OF MY SON...
...HAS FILTHY BLOOD.
I HAVE NEVER GIVEN MY HEART TO A WOMAN...
...BECAUSE THE WORLD IS LITTERED WITH WOMEN.

SO...
WAS THIS ALSO A RESULT OF YOUR DECEITFUL MAGIC? DID YOU STEAL MY HEART AWAY?!
WELL?! SAY SOMETHING!!

티잉
하아
하아
하아
하아
하아

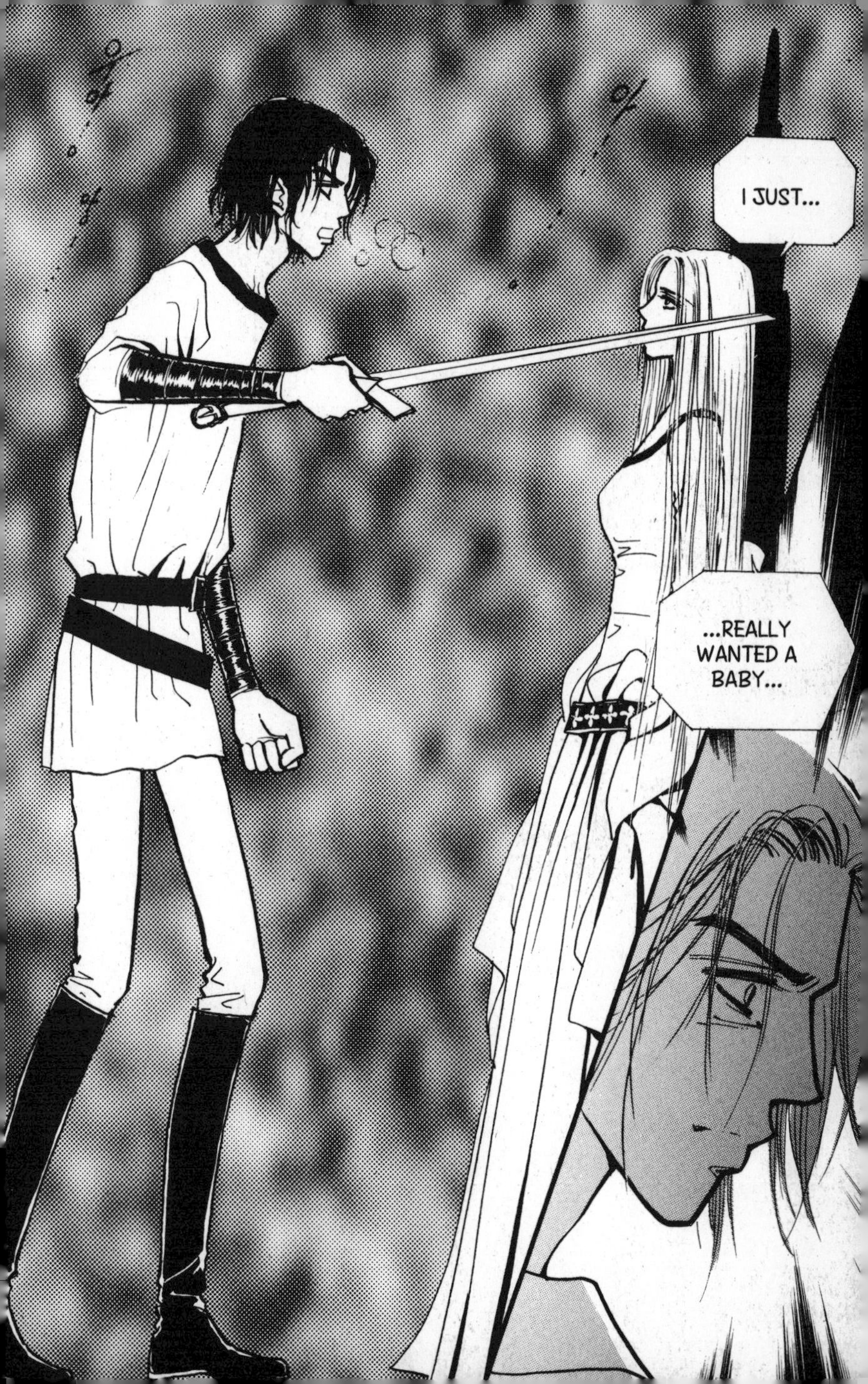
I JUST...
...REALLY WANTED A BABY...

THAT'S ALL YOU HAVE TO SAY FOR YOURSELF?!
THAT YOU WANTED A BABY...?!

GET OUT OF MY WAY!
DO YOU REALLY THINK I'M GOING TO LET A MONSTER WITH WITCH'S BLOOD LIVE?!

NOOOOOOO

O!!

번쩍
휘르르르르...

WAAAAHHHH...
WAAAAHHHH...

MY BABY...
MY DARLING BABY...
WAAAAHHH...
WAAAAHHH...

FROM NOW ON, I'LL MAKE IT SO THAT NO ONE CAN **EVER** HURT YOU OR EVEN TRY TO KILL YOU!

NO ONE WILL EVER BE ABLE TO TAKE YOUR LIFE... EVEN IF I HAVE TO BORROW THE STRENGTH OF THE BLACK ARTS OR USE SORCERY...

I'M GOING TO ENSURE THAT NO ONE WILL EVER BE ABLE TO KILL YOU!!
NO ONE KNEW THE SPECIFICS ABOUT THE DEATH OF RIENO GROSS, NOR DID THEY KNOW ANYTHING ABOUT HIS WIFE AND SON.
THE QUEEN EVENTUALLY FOUND A NEW LOVE...

BUT THE VILLAGE OF DUNKKAR CONTINUED TO FALL TO RUIN. RUMORS BEGAN TO SPREAD THAT THE LORD OF DUNKKAR WAS NO LONGER CONCERNED ABOUT RULING THE VILLAGE...
EVEN ALL THE CITIZENS BEGAN TO MOVE TO OTHER VILLAGES.
THE VILLAGE OF DUNKKAR FELL DEEPER INTO DARKNESS...UNTIL IT SOON BECAME A WASTELAND. EVER SO SLOWLY, IT FADED FROM PEOPLE'S MEMORIES...

IN THIS WAY, TIME PASSED...
HA HA HA HA HA HA!
HA HA HA HA HA HA!

WHEN WILL THE QUEEN'S QUEST FOR LOVE COME TO AN END?
SHE'S CHANGED LOVERS YET AGAIN... I WONDER HOW LONG THIS ONE WILL LAST?
SHE HAS NO INTENTION TO MARRY...
HMPH! I'M NOT USED TO WOMEN CHEATING ON THEIR MEN...
WELL, BECAUSE OF HER, SPRING DOESN'T LOOK LIKE IT'LL END ANYTIME SOON, DOES IT?
BUT I SUPPOSE THAT'S TRUE...
THE PAST SEVERAL YEARS' PEACEFUL CALM MAKES ME UNEASY FOR SOME REASON...
MAYBE I'M JUST BEING A WORRYWART...?
WHY DO I KEEP GETTING THIS STRANGE, FOREBODING FEELING...?

SEVERAL YEARS AGO THAT ILL-FATED SIGN ON THAT OMINOUS NIGHT... WHY DID IT DISAPPEAR ALL OF A SUDDEN?
WAS THE PROPHESY OF THE CHILD OF DARKNESS WRONG?
ALL THE WISE MEN CAME TOGETHER IN AGREEMENT, BUT...
WHAT IN THE WORLD HAPPENED?
HAVE YOU HEARD THE RUMORS, YOUR MAJESTY?

THERE'S SOMEONE WHO HAS SEEN RIENO GROSS, THE LORD OF DUNKKAR VILLAGE AROUND THAT AREA.

AH! THE QUEEN IS TAKING AN INTEREST!

GO FIND OUT IF THE RUMORS ARE TRUE! EVEN IF IT IS A GHOST...
...I WILL NOT FORGIVE THE SPREADING OF SUCH RUMORS!
YES, YOUR HIGHNESS.

WHOA...!
WHOA, NOW...!

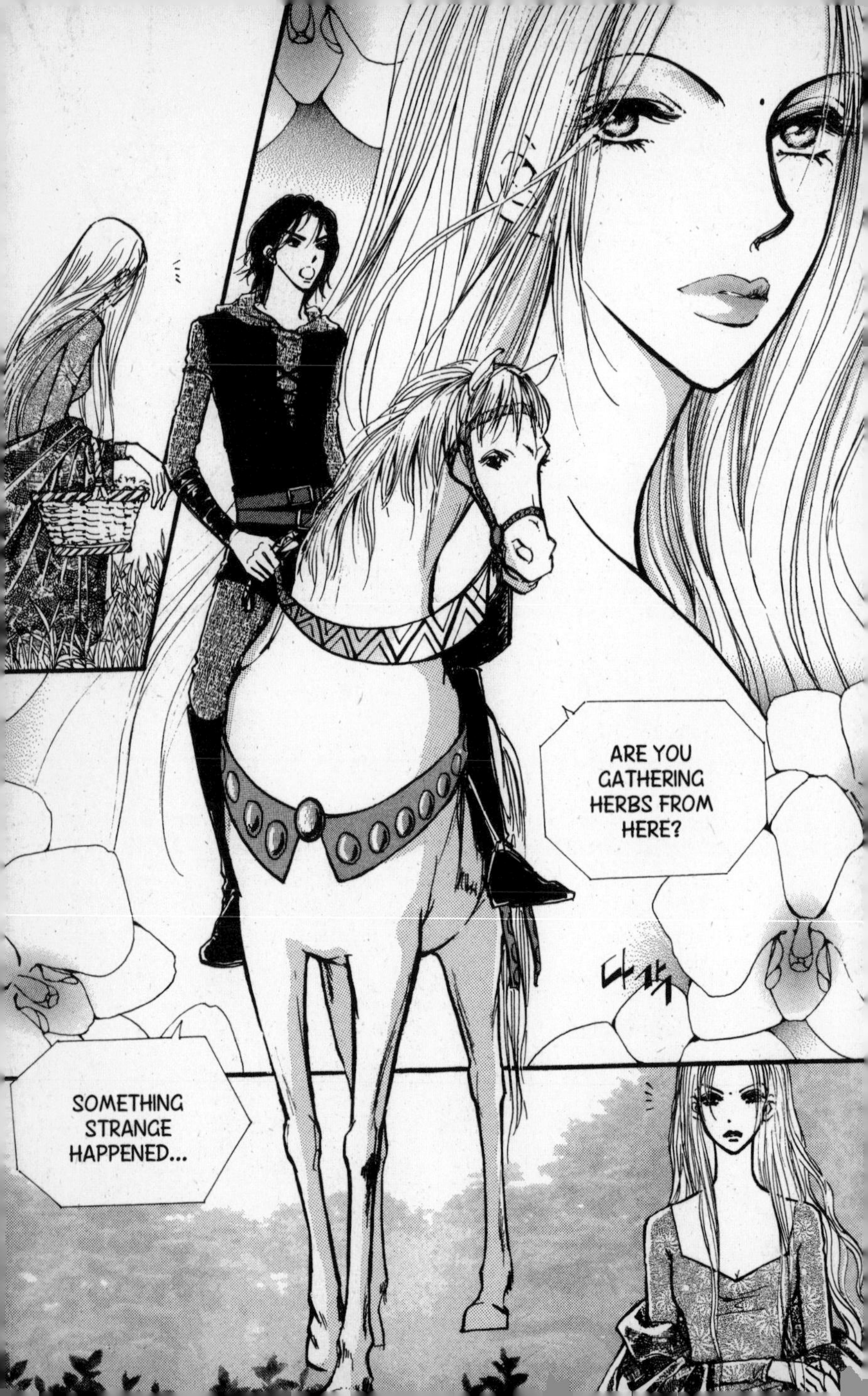
ARE YOU GATHERING HERBS FROM HERE?
SOMETHING STRANGE HAPPENED...

PEOPLE ARE COMING TO THE CASTLE...
HEAR YE! BY ORDER OF THE QUEEN!

BY ORDER OF THE QUEEN...
...THE QUEEN...
...THE QUEEN...
BY ORDER OF THE QUEEN...
IT'S LIKE A HAUNTED CASTLE...!
조용
COME OUT QUICKLY AND RECEIVE THE ORDER!
조용
COMMANDER, LOOK!!

WHO ARE YOU?! AND WHERE IS THE LORD OF DUNKKAR, RIENO GROSS?!
WHAT? HE'S JUST A KID?!
WHERE IS THE MASTER OF THE CASTLE?
I AM THE MASTER.
THE RUMORS MUST BE TRUE...! THE LORD DIED...AND HIS SON TOOK OVER...

HMPH.
LET'S GO!

IT ANNOUNCES THE OPENING OF THE TOURNAMENT.
AND IT SAYS THAT YOU MUST PARTICIPATE IN ORDER TO BE ACKNOWLEDGED AS THE NEW MASTER OF DUNKKAR AND THIS CASTLE.
HEXE--I'VE NEVER FOUGHT AGAINST A HUMAN BEING BEFORE.

SURE, I'VE SWUNG MY SWORD A FEW TIMES AGAINST MONSTERS AND EVIL SPIRITS BECAUSE THEY ALWAYS COME AFTER ME, BUT...
I'LL READY YOUR ARMOR AND MAKE PREPARATIONS FOR YOUR JOURNEY.
HEY! ARE YOU SAYING THAT I SHOULD ACTUALLY OBEY THIS ORDER?!
RIENO...

ONE DAY, I WILL LEAVE...AND YOU WILL BE ON YOUR OWN.
THANKS TO THE DARK BLOOD THAT FLOWS THROUGH YOUR BODY, YOU WILL NOT BE EASILY SWEPT AWAY BY LONELINESS OR EMPTY EMOTIONS.
YOU HAVE A HEART COLDER THAN THE DARKEST WINTER MORN.
HOWEVER...

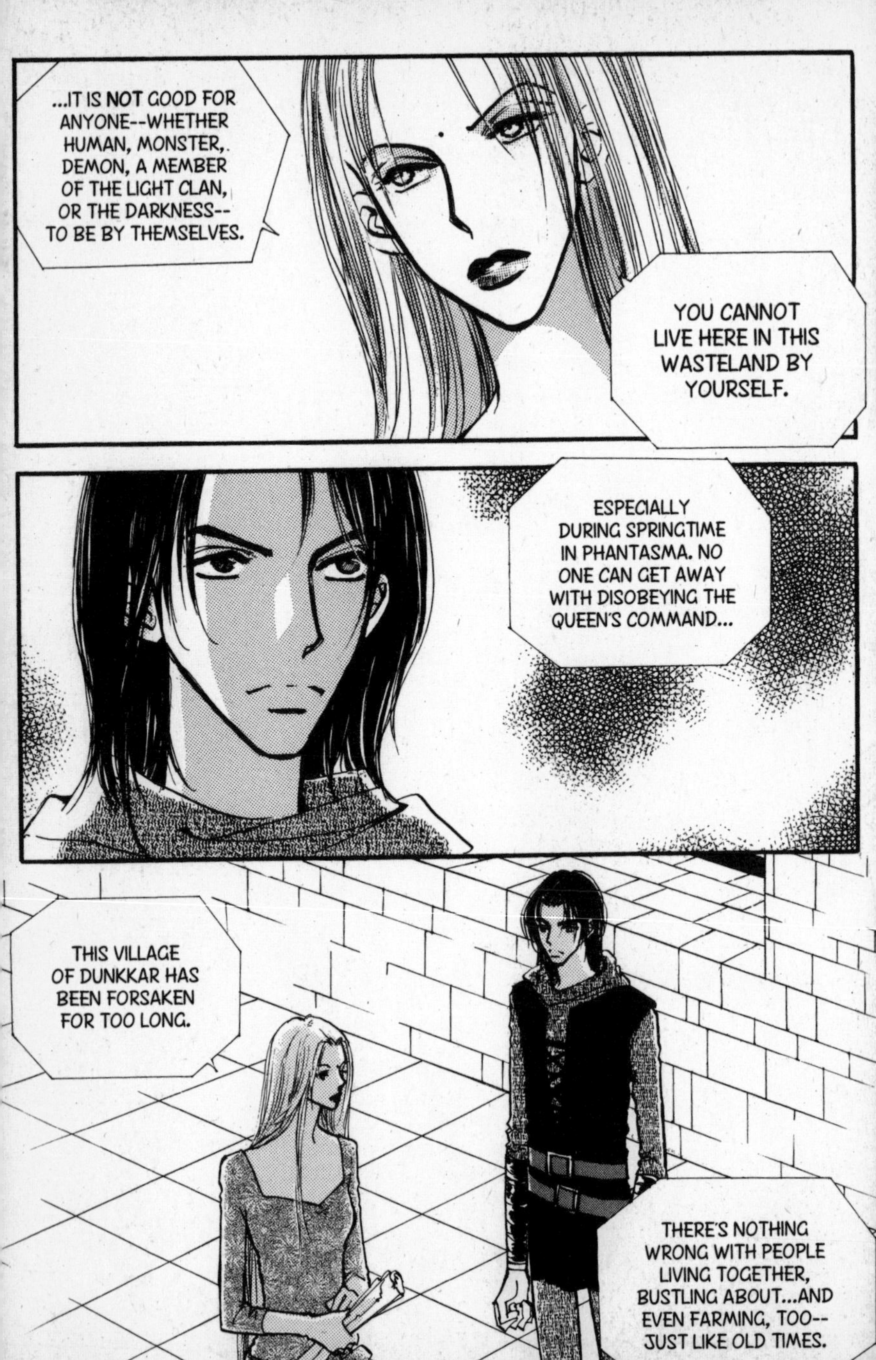
...IT IS NOT GOOD FOR ANYONE--WHETHER HUMAN, MONSTER, DEMON, A MEMBER OF THE LIGHT CLAN, OR THE DARKNESS-- TO BE BY THEMSELVES.
YOU CANNOT LIVE HERE IN THIS WASTELAND BY YOURSELF.
ESPECIALLY DURING SPRINGTIME IN PHANTASMA. NO ONE CAN GET AWAY WITH DISOBEYING THE QUEEN'S COMMAND...
THIS VILLAGE OF DUNKKAR HAS BEEN FORSAKEN FOR TOO LONG.
THERE'S NOTHING WRONG WITH PEOPLE LIVING TOGETHER, BUSTLING ABOUT...AND EVEN FARMING, TOO-- JUST LIKE OLD TIMES.

THIS IS SOMETHING INCOMPREHENSIBLE TO THE OLD ME...
......
I CAN'T BELIEVE THAT I ACTUALLY FEAR LONELINESS...

THAT BOY, RIENO...
...RESEMBLES HIM MORE WITH EVERY PASSING DAY.
RIENO GROSS...
HMM... THE QUEEN WILL CALL FOR RIENO AND TRY TO KILL HIM.
AND THEN...

...WILL IT BE
MY TURN?
I'VE USED ALL
OF MY ENERGY...
...TRYING TO
PROTECT THAT BOY
FROM THE POWER
OF DARKNESS.
BUT SOON, EVEN
MY ENERGY WILL
HIT ROCK BOTTOM.

THE ENERGY SURROUNDING THIS CASTLE AND DUNKKAR VILLAGE GROWS WEAKER AND WEAKER...
THERE ARE VULNERABLE AREAS HERE AND THERE... AND I CAN NO LONGER BAR PEOPLE FROM ENTERING...

IN A LITTLE WHILE, THE WORLD WILL BECOME CONSCIOUS OF THIS LITTLE BOY CALLED RIENO...

IF I CAN NO LONGER PROTECT HIM FROM THE POWERS OF LIGHT AND DARKNESS...
...THEN I SHOULD SEND HIM OUT. I'VE DONE ALL I CAN FOR HIM...

ACK!

WHAT IN THE WORLD--?! HOW CAN THAT BE...?!
웅성
THAT KID JUST DEFEATED SOME OF OUR TOP KNIGHTS!
웅성
웅성
웅성
THEN THE RUMORS MUST BE TRUE! HE IS INDEED THE SON OF RIENO GROSS!
웅성
RIENO'S SON AND THE WOMAN WHO BORE HIM WILL BOTH DIE--THIS, I SWEAR!
LOOK OVER THERE!

THE FINAL COMPETITION IS BETWEEN THE QUEEN'S GREATEST KNIGHT, HERMANN, FROM THE HOHU VILLAGE...
...AND THE DANGEROUS HERO RIENO OF DUNKKAR, WHO IS TAKING PART IN OUR TOURNAMENT FOR THE VERY FIRST TIME.
DAMN, HE'S HUGE...!
KILL HIM, HERMANN!!
HERMANN IS THE BEST...!
HERMANN!
DURING THE TOURNAMENT, I WANT YOU TO DRIVE YOUR SWORD INTO RIENO'S HEART. YOU MUSTN'T FAIL!
SO SHE WANTS ME TO KILL THIS LITTLE KID... HMPH. HER MAJESTY SURE HAS SOME STRANGE PREFERENCES.

RAAH!!
HEH... PRETTY GOOD.
BY THE GODS, HE'S STRONG!

HERMANN...!
HERMANN...!
HERMANN...!
THIS IS NO JOKE...! THIS KID MAY BE AN AMATEUR, BUT HE SURE DOESN'T FIGHT LIKE IT!
HUFF!
HUFF!
HUFF
HUFF!
HUFF!
HUFF!
CRAP! I CAN'T BELIEVE I'M GETTING DESPERATE!!
...!
YAAAAH!!

ACK!
I'VE STABBED HIS HEART!!

HERMENY
BROTHER!!
ALLOW ME TO RETURN THE FAVOR...
......
HUFF!
HUFF!

THIS WAY...!!
BLOOD STAINS! DON'T LOSE HER! THIS WAY!!
SEARCH EVERY-WHERE!
AS SOON AS YOU FIND THE WOMAN, KILL HER!
...
IT'S A ROYAL DECREE! YOU MUST FIND HER AND KILL HER!

HEXE...WE FINALLY MEET!
......
WHO...?
WHO WOULD HAVE THOUGHT THAT YOUR MAGIC WOULD BE GREAT ENOUGH TO SHIELD THE WHOLE OF DUNKKAR VILLAGE...?
THAT'S PROBABLY WHY WE COULDN'T FIND YOU FOR SO MANY YEARS.
......
......
WE'VE FOUND HER!
FOUND HER!

WHY ARE YOU BEING CHASED OUT OF THE PALACE BY THE QUEEN'S SOLDIERS?
WE'VE COME TO PUT YOU ON TRIAL.
......
WHAT IS IT?

WE'VE TRIED THREE TIMES, BUT HE DOESN'T SHOW ANY RESPONSE AT ALL.
THE POISON DOESN'T SEEM TO HAVE ANY EFFECT ON HIM EITHER...
THAT MAN RIENO APPEARS TO BE INVINCIBLE...
EVEN DURING THE TOURNAMENT, WHEN HERMANN STABBED HIM IN THE HEART...
...RIENO SAYS THAT HERMANN MISSED AND STABBED HIM **NEAR** HIS HEART...BUT THAT'S HARD TO BELIEVE.
ON TOP OF THAT, THESE DAYS, EVEN THE QUEEN FINDS HIM IN HER FAVOR...
CHANCELLOR HWERUSUTE!

I HEARD THAT THE QUEEN INTENDS TO RESTORE THE LAND AND THE POSITION OF THE LATE RIENO GROSS TO HIS SON!
ARE THE RUMORS TRUE? IS RIENO GOING TO BE APPOINTED IN HERMANN'S STEAD...
...AS THE QUEEN'S NEW KNIGHT?!
COLD EYES...
YOU HAVE THE EYES OF A BEAST--ROUGH AND UNTAMED. SUCH A COLD GAZE...

SAW EYES LIKE THIS...
I'M NOT INTERESTED. NOW THAT I'VE FULLY RECOVERED FROM MY WOUND, I SIMPLY WANT TO RETURN TO DUNKKAR VILLAGE.
DO YOU KNOW WHAT I WANT TO DO WITH YOU?
HMM...
LIKE FATHER, LIKE SON...
BUT...
HEE HEE HEE...

...HMM!
GULP!
WH-
WHAT WAS
THAT...?!
I SWALLOWED
SOMETHING...!

IT'S A LOVE POTION.
A POTION THAT WILL MAKE YOU FALL IN LOVE.
THOSE COLD EYES WILL NOW LOOK AT ME AND BURN WITH PASSION.
YOU'LL BURN... AND BURN. YOU'LL ONLY HAVE EYES FOR ME...ALWAYS...
.....
YOU'LL STRUGGLE BETWEEN SUFFERING AND DELIGHT, AND BE CONSUMED WITH PASSION!

HMM...I'VE HEARD OF YOUR BAD HABITS REGARDING MEN...
GULP!

……
스윽
……
풀썩
저벅
저벅
저벅
저벅…

웅성
웅성
웅성
RIENO...

AS THE WATER MIRROR REVEALS, POTIONS DON'T SEEM TO HAVE ANY EFFECT ON THE WITCH'S SON.
THEN WHAT SHOULD WE DO?
MUST WE REALLY RESORT TO SUCH RECKLESS ACTS?

NO ONE CAN EVER HARM THAT BOY...
BUT, I WANTED TO PROTECT HIM UNTIL HE REACHED THE AGE OF NINETEEN.
I'VE GROWN SO WEAK FROM TRYING TO PROTECT HIM FROM THE EVIL POWERS OF THAT THING...
PHANTASMA IS A WORLD THAT EXISTS UPON THE DELICATE BALANCE BETWEEN DARKNESS AND LIGHT.
FINALLY...WE HAD COME TO REALIZE THE OBJECT OF OUR FEAR THROUGH HEXE'S TRIAL!
ALTHOUGH HEXE DIDN'T SPEAK OF IT HERSELF, WE COULD CONFIRM IT THE MOMENT WE SAW RIENO! THE WITCH HAD GIVEN BIRTH TO AND RAISED...

...THE SUCCESSOR TO THE THRONE OF DARKNESS THAT APPEARED SEVERAL YEARS AGO!!
THE PROPHESY WAS INDEED TRUE...

WE CANNOT BLOCK HIM WITH OUR STRENGTH.
ON TOP OF THAT, HE IS NOW SEVENTEEN YEARS OLD.
THROUGH HEXE'S MAGIC AND THE POWER OF DARKNESS, HIS BODY HAS BECOME ALMOST INVINCIBLE.
WE CANNOT DETECT A WEAKNESS.
BUT WE CAN'T JUST SIT IDLY BY UNTIL RIENO TURNS NINETEEN...!

WORLD OF LIGHT! IN PHANTASMA DURING THIS DRAWN-OUT SPRINGTIME...
...THE POWERS OF DARKNESS WILL TAKE THIS OPPORTUNITY TO GAIN STRENGTH...
다각
다각
다각
다각
다각
히이이이이...!
WE MUST GET RID OF RIENO!
IF WE DO NOT STOP HIM, THE ONLY FUTURE PHANTASMA WILL HAVE IS ONE OF ETERNAL DARKNESS.

HEXE...?
THIS IS THE END OF SPRING IN PHANTASMA...
HEXE?
HEXE?!
IF THAT HAPPENS, THE LIGHT CLAN WILL HAVE NOWHERE TO GO...
HEXE!

WE CANNOT
JUST WATCH...
...AS THE WITCH'S
SON, RIENO...

THAT BOY... THE VESSEL OF OUR DOOM...
...AWAKENS TO THE POWERS OF DARKNESS INSIDE HIM.
......

...MUST NEVER COME TO RULE PHANTASMA AS LORD OF DARKNESS!!
HEXE...

IF WE CANNOT STOP HIM WITH OUR STRENGTH...
...UNTIL WE CAN COME UP WITH A METHOD...
...UNTIL WE CAN DISCOVER RIENO'S WEAKNESS...
...UNTIL THEN, WE WILL STOP TIME IN PHANTASMA.
WE MUST KILL HIM BEFORE THAT DESIRE AWAKENS INSIDE HIM!!

BY THE REQUEST OF THE FAIRY KING, WHO IS THE GUARDIAN OF THE LIGHT CLAN...
...I SENT THE QUEEN A LOVE POTION.
AS EXPECTED, IT DID NOT HAVE ANY EFFECT ON RIENO...
IN THE WATER MIRROR, WE JUST SAW THE QUEEN AND RIENO TAKING IT.
SO, EHREN...?
QUEEN FREYJA LOST ALL CONTROL AFTERWARD BECAUSE OF THAT POTION.

THE POTION WILL CAUSE THE QUEEN TO GO MAD WITH BURNING PASSION. IN ORDER TO PREVENT RIENO'S MATURATION...
...WE'LL CALL FORTH WINTER TO PHANTASMA.
......
THAT WAS SOMETHING THAT NO ONE EXCEPT THE QUEEN COULD HAVE DONE...

HOWEVER, IF SPRING CONTINUES, RIENO WILL TRANSFORM.
YOU REALLY ARE SOMETHING! YOU TOO, HEMEL...!
EVEN THE LIGHT CLAN!!
HOW COULD YOU HAVE KEPT THIS A SECRET UNTIL NOW?!
SO JUST WHAT IS IT THAT YOU WANT TO SAY TO YUNA AND I?!
TO BE CONTINUED IN VOLUME 9

IN SEARCH OF PHANTASMA...

PHANTASMA? ISN'T THAT THE PLACE YOU GO TO MEET RIENO?

AUTHOR

IT'S BEEN A LONG TIME SINCE I LAST GREW OUT MY HAIR.

YEAH, THAT'S TRUE, BUT...

...I'M THINKING OF TELLING A DIFFERENT STORY THIS TIME...

THE LOCATION OF PHANTASMA, THE NAMES AND MODELS THAT WERE USED IN THE STORY...

PHANTASMA WAS INSPIRED BY A SMALL REGION NEAR THE SOUTH OF GERMANY NAMED FÜSSEN.

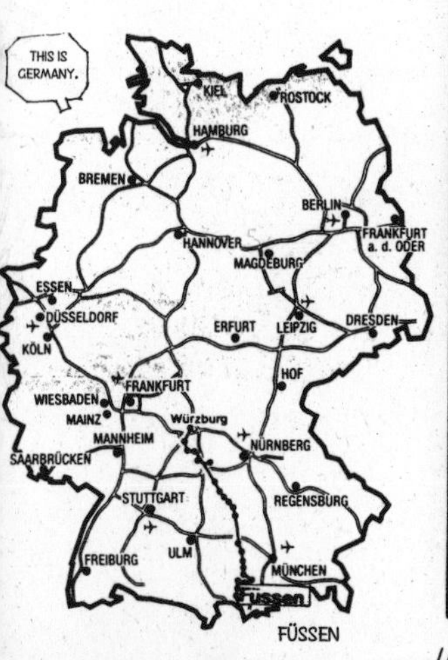

FÜSSEN

FÜSSEN IS NEAR THE AUSTRIAN BORDER, AT THE FOOT OF THE BAVARIAN ALPS. ITS ALTITUDE IS 800 METERS. IT IS A ROMANTIC CITY WITH LOTS OF MOUNTAINS AND LAKES.

THIS IS THE ENTRANCE TO NEUSCHWANSTEIN CASTLE. YOU NEED TO WALK ALL THE WAY UP THE MOUNTAIN TO GET THERE. YUNA CAME HERE ALSO!

I COULDN'T FIND A PICTURE THAT COULD DO FÜSSEN JUSTICE IN DEPICTING ITS TRUE BEAUTY... I JUST HAD TO SETTLE FOR ONE OF MY OLD TRAVEL PHOTOS.

FOUR KILOMETERS AWAY FROM FÜSSEN IS THE SCHUBANKOU FOREST. ON A CLIFF IS A FAIRY TALE CASTLE THAT WAS BUILT BY THE LAST EMPEROR OF GERMANY, KING LUDWIG II, AND CALLED NEUSCHWANSTEIN CASTLE--OR SWAN CASTLE.
KING LUDWIG II WAS A GREAT FAN OF WAGNER. HE FELL IN LOVE WITH THE IMAGE OF SWANS BECAUSE OF WAGNER. IN THE CASTLE, THERE ARE MANY IMAGES OF SWANS HERE AND THERE.
IN ADDITION, THERE ARE MANY MURALS WITHIN THE CASTLE ITSELF THAT ARE BASED UPON THE LEGENDS WAGNER USED IN HIS OPERAS, SUCH AS "DER RING DES NIBELUNGEN," "TRISTAN UND ISOLDE," "PARSIFAL," AND "TANNHÄUSER," ETC.

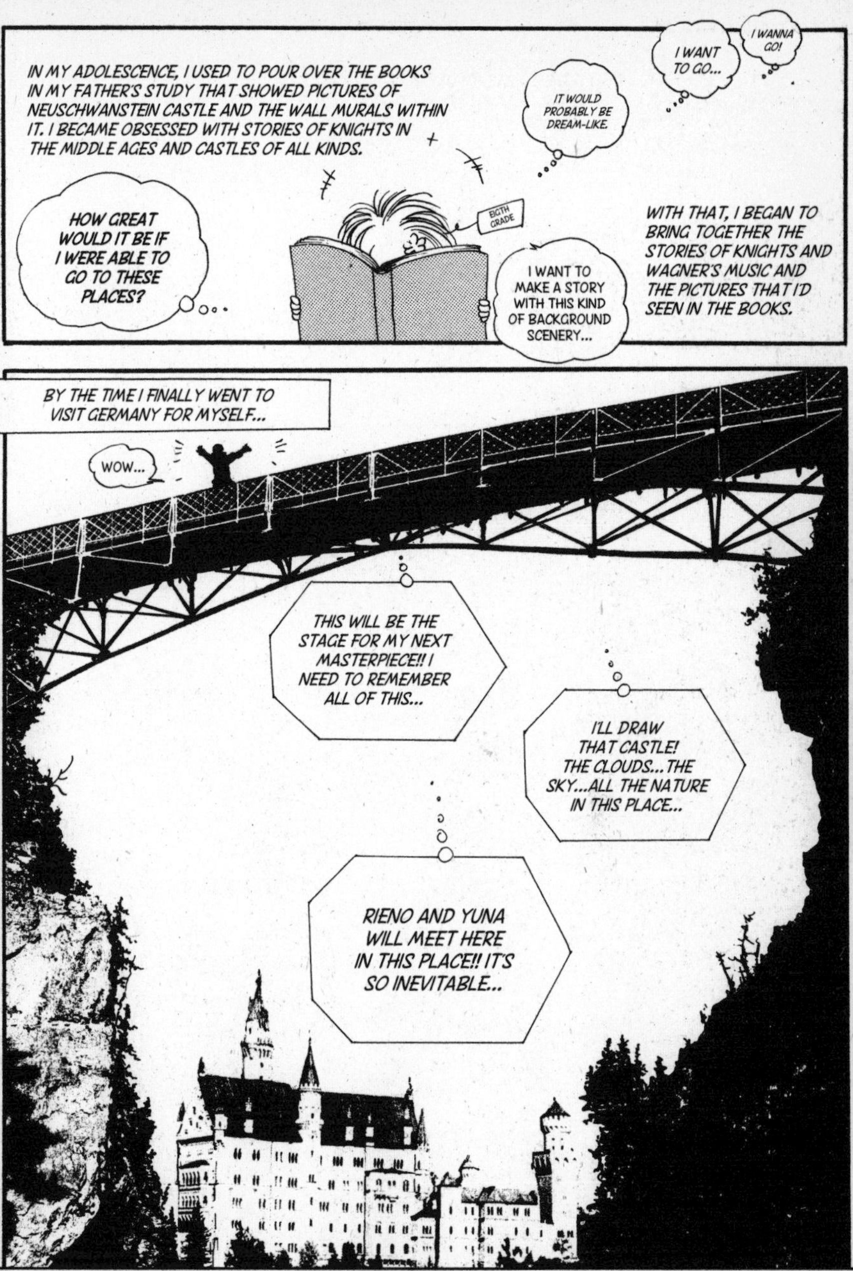
IN MY ADOLESCENCE, I USED TO POUR OVER THE BOOKS IN MY FATHER'S STUDY THAT SHOWED PICTURES OF NEUSCHWANSTEIN CASTLE AND THE WALL MURALS WITHIN IT. I BECAME OBSESSED WITH STORIES OF KNIGHTS IN THE MIDDLE AGES AND CASTLES OF ALL KINDS.
IT WOULD PROBABLY BE DREAM-LIKE.
I WANT TO GO...
I WANNA GO!
HOW GREAT WOULD IT BE IF I WERE ABLE TO GO TO THESE PLACES?
EIGTH GRADE
I WANT TO MAKE A STORY WITH THIS KIND OF BACKGROUND SCENERY...
WITH THAT, I BEGAN TO BRING TOGETHER THE STORIES OF KNIGHTS AND WAGNER'S MUSIC AND THE PICTURES THAT I'D SEEN IN THE BOOKS.
BY THE TIME I FINALLY WENT TO VISIT GERMANY FOR MYSELF...
WOW...
THIS WILL BE THE STAGE FOR MY NEXT MASTERPIECE!! I NEED TO REMEMBER ALL OF THIS...
I'LL DRAW THAT CASTLE! THE CLOUDS...THE SKY...ALL THE NATURE IN THIS PLACE...
RIENO AND YUNA WILL MEET HERE IN THIS PLACE!! IT'S SO INEVITABLE...
IF YOU WALK UP A LITTLE FURTHER FROM NEUSCHWANSTEIN CASTLE, YOU REACH A RIVER GORGE CALLED PÖLLAT. ABOVE THAT GORGE IS THE MARIEN BRIDGE. WHEN YOU STAND THERE AND TAKE IN THE CASTLE, THE LAKE, THE SURROUNDING VILLAGES, CLOUDS, AND THE SKY, THERE IS NO GREATER SCENIC MASTERPIECE.

THE VILLAGE OF DUNKKAR, OF WHICH RIENO IS LORD, IS BASED ON A SMALL VILLAGE SURROUNDING NEUSCHWANSTEIN CASTLE (EVEN THOUGH IN THE STORY, DUNKKAR IS NOWHERE NEAR A CLIFF AND STONES).

MAP OF GERMANY

IT IS VERY SIMILAR TO THE MAP OF PHANTASMA THAT I DREW, ISN'T IT? (LAUGHTER)

MAP OF PHANTASMA

THIS MEANS THAT PHANTASMA IS BASED IN THE REGION OF FÜSSEN AND ITS SURROUNDING AREAS, BUT IN A DIFFERENT DIMENSION.

I WONDER IF THEY'LL KNOW THAT I'M A GUY IF I LOOK LIKE THIS.

THESE DAYS, THE AUTHOR'S HAIR IS LONG.

PAST IMAGE.

OOH-- IT'S TOO DIFFICULT...

SORRY...! IF I WERE TO EXPLAIN IT ONE MORE TIME...

TONE POWDER.

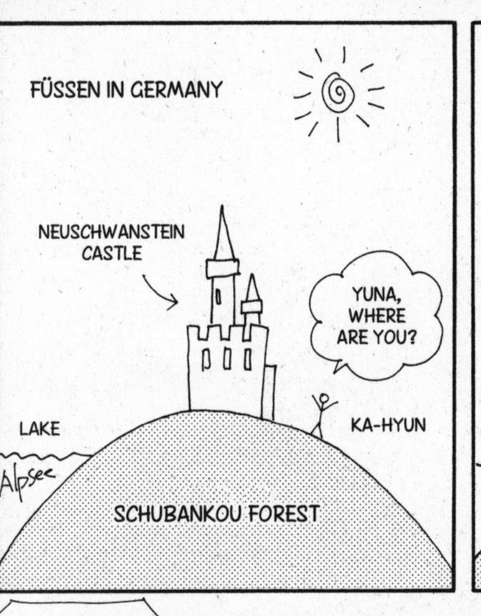

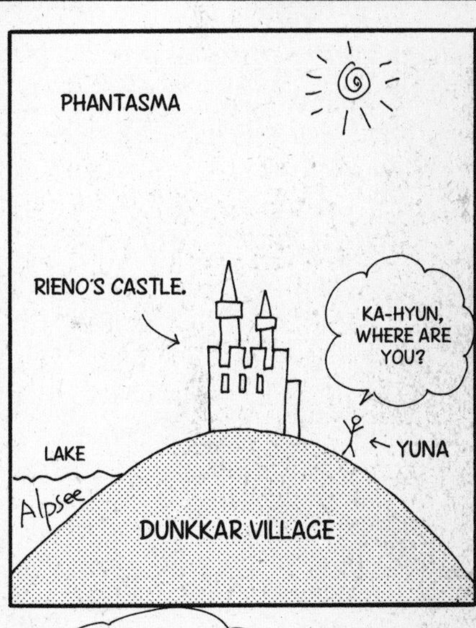

YUNA--SORRY. YOU GOTTA ASK RIENO THAT. I DON'T KNOW...
ojoj~
THAT BASTARD WON'T TELL ME...!

THAT'S TRUE!

AH! EHREN! ♡

GASP! TWO AGAINST ONE...! THIS DOES NOT BODE WELL FOR ME! ON TOP OF THAT, GOING UP AGAINST THIS GUY...

THAT'S WHY...

...ORIGINALLY, PHANTASMA WAS A WORLD OF BALANCE BETWEEN LIGHT AND DARKNESS.

LET'S CHANGE THE SUBJECT SO THAT IT'S MORE FAVORABLE FOR ME.

AFTER THE QUEEN WAS SELECTED FROM THE LINE OF FAIRIES OF THE LIGHT CLAN...

ONCE SPRING LASTED FOR LONG PERIODS OF TIME, THE POWERS OF DARKNESS WERE GREATLY DIMINISHED, AND INSTEAD, LIGHT POWER (DENSITY) INCREASED TREMENDOUSLY.

Density = Mass / Volume

IN TERMS OF PHYSICS, THE MASS REMAINED THE SAME, BUT SINCE THE VOLUME DECREASED, THE DENSITY INCREASED ALL THE MORE.

BUT, WHY? WHY DID THE QUEEN ONLY ASSOCIATE WITH THE LIGHT CLAN?

DON'T YOU THINK IT'S BECAUSE LOVE AND RELATIONSHIPS ARE MORE CHARACTERISTIC OF THE LIGHT CLAN?

HONESTLY, I DON'T REALLY KNOW FOR SURE MYSELF.

THAT'S RIGHT...! I CAN TELL WHEN I LOOK AT RIENO!

HOW IS IT POSSIBLE FOR HER TO SAY THAT WHEN SHE DOESN'T KNOW RIENO'S TRUE IDENTITY?

THE AUTHOR SURE IS STUPID...

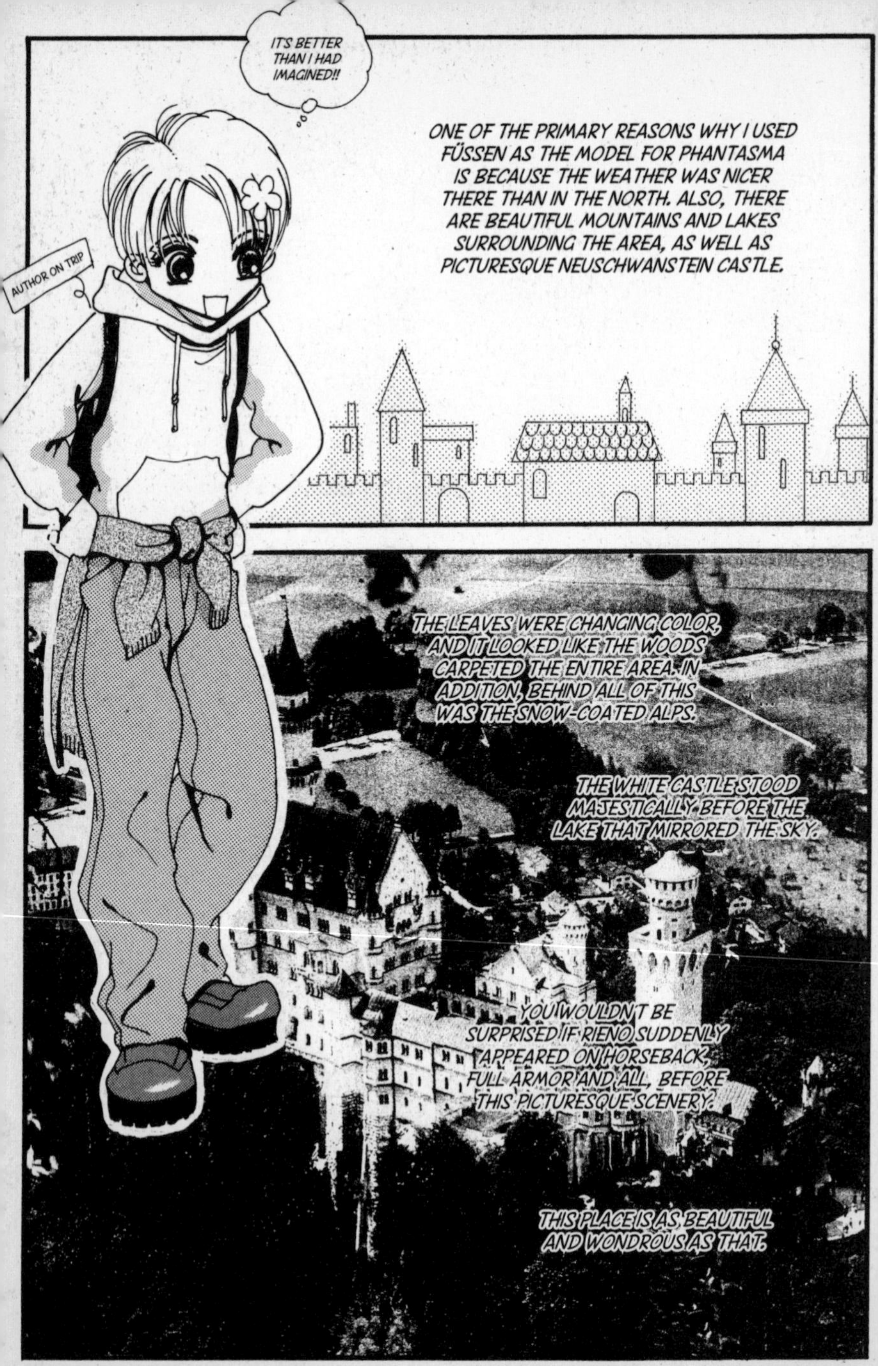

IT'S BETTER THAN I HAD IMAGINED!!
ONE OF THE PRIMARY REASONS WHY I USED FÜSSEN AS THE MODEL FOR PHANTASMA IS BECAUSE THE WEATHER WAS NICER THERE THAN IN THE NORTH. ALSO, THERE ARE BEAUTIFUL MOUNTAINS AND LAKES SURROUNDING THE AREA, AS WELL AS PICTURESQUE NEUSCHWANSTEIN CASTLE.
AUTHOR ON TRIP
THE LEAVES WERE CHANGING COLOR, AND IT LOOKED LIKE THE WOODS CARPETED THE ENTIRE AREA. IN ADDITION, BEHIND ALL OF THIS WAS THE SNOW-COATED ALPS.
THE WHITE CASTLE STOOD MAJESTICALLY BEFORE THE LAKE THAT MIRRORED THE SKY.
YOU WOULDN'T BE SURPRISED IF RIENO SUDDENLY APPEARED ON HORSEBACK, FULL ARMOR AND ALL, BEFORE THIS PICTURESQUE SCENERY.
THIS PLACE IS AS BEAUTIFUL AND WONDROUS AS THAT.

THE MOTIF FOR THE STORY OF RIENO AND HEXE WAS INSPIRED BY MECANO'S "HIJO DE LA LUNA." ♫

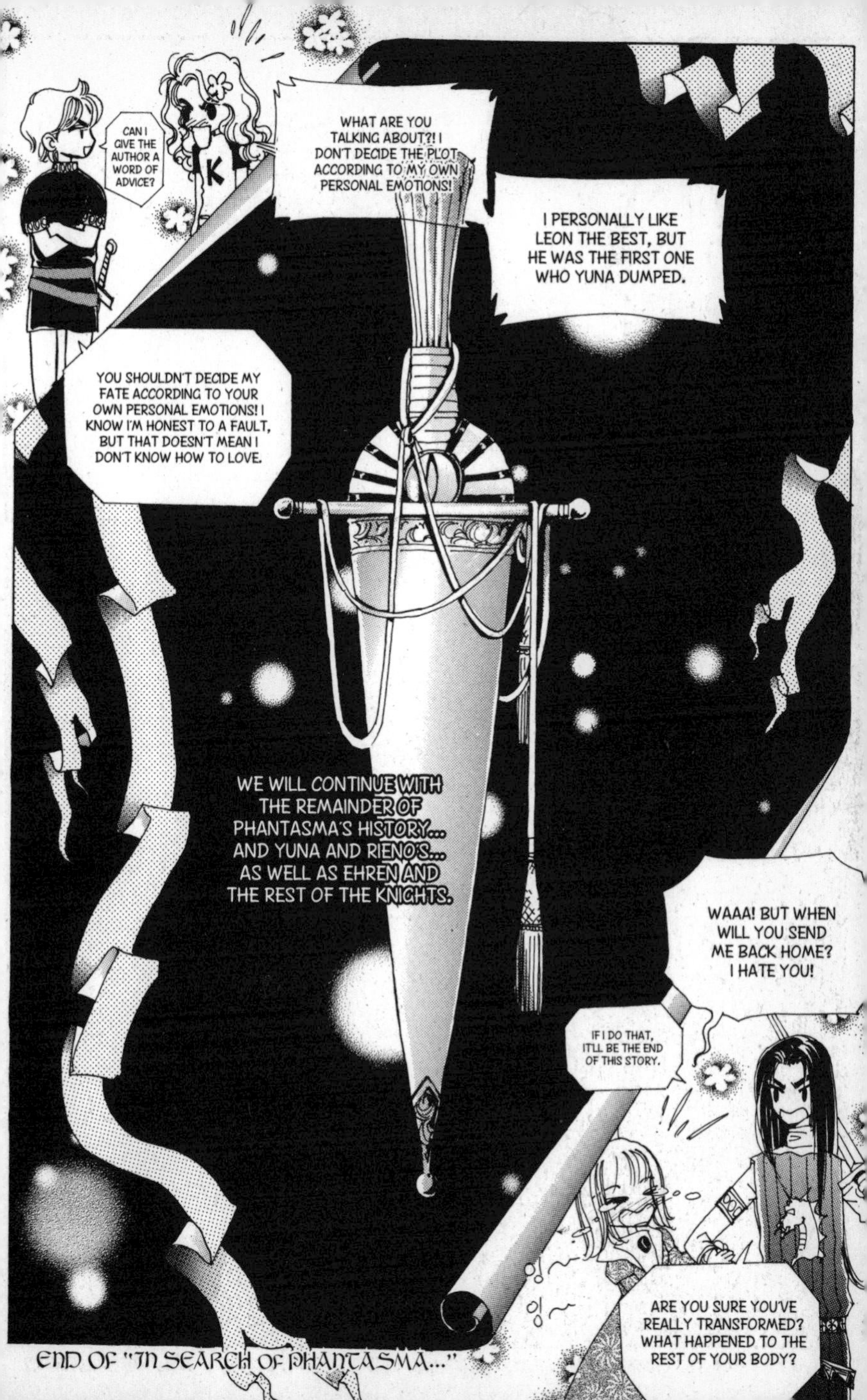
CAN I GIVE THE AUTHOR A WORD OF ADVICE?
WHAT ARE YOU TALKING ABOUT?! I DON'T DECIDE THE PLOT ACCORDING TO MY OWN PERSONAL EMOTIONS!
I PERSONALLY LIKE LEON THE BEST, BUT HE WAS THE FIRST ONE WHO YUNA DUMPED.
YOU SHOULDN'T DECIDE MY FATE ACCORDING TO YOUR OWN PERSONAL EMOTIONS! I KNOW I'M HONEST TO A FAULT, BUT THAT DOESN'T MEAN I DON'T KNOW HOW TO LOVE.
WE WILL CONTINUE WITH THE REMAINDER OF PHANTASMA'S HISTORY... AND YUNA AND RIENO'S... AS WELL AS EHREN AND THE REST OF THE KNIGHTS.
WAAA! BUT WHEN WILL YOU SEND ME BACK HOME? I HATE YOU!
IF I DO THAT, IT'LL BE THE END OF THIS STORY.
ARE YOU SURE YOU'VE REALLY TRANSFORMED? WHAT HAPPENED TO THE REST OF YOUR BODY?
END OF "IN SEARCH OF PHANTASMA..."

IN THE NEXT VOLUME OF...

THE QUEEN'S KNIGHT

WHILE YUNA CONTINUES TO BE AT A LOSS AS TO THE IDENTITY OF THE PERSON OF HER AFFECTIONS, SHE IS BRIEFLY ABLE TO FORGET HER WOES VIA A COSTUME BALL. HOWEVER, WHEN REINO STORMS IN AND CARRIES HER AWAY, IT WORKS THE KNIGHTS INTO A FRENZY...BUT EVEN MORE UPSETTING FOR YUNA IS THAT SOON AFTER THIS EVENT HER HAIR GROWS YET AGAIN. THIS ALL SUGGESTS THAT PERHAPS REINO IS INDEED HER HEART'S DESIRE...BUT AT WHAT COST?

COMING SOON!

CHOOSE
YOUR
MANGA
WITH ATTITUDE!
TOKYOPOP
UTOPIA'S AVENGER
CREATED BY OH SE-KWON 1
Check out www.TOKYOPOP.com and
www.ChooseWeapon.com for more details.

WEAPON
THE MANGA REVOLUTION · LEADING · THE MANGA REVOLUTION · LEADING
漫画革命
GYAKUSHU!
TOKYOPOP
HIPP 1
ARCHLORD
1
JIN-HWAN PARK
PHANTOM
TOKYOPOP
PICK UP YOUR
SAMPLER AT
FREE COMIC
BOOK DAY.

TRINITY BLOOD

BY SUNAO YOSHIDA, KIYO KYUJO AND THORES SHIBAMOTO

In a dark and distant future, Armageddon has giving rise to a perpetual war between the vampires and the humans! The nun Esther crosses paths with Abel Nightroad, a priest, to form a holy alliance and battle the most evil of threats!

ACTION | OT OLDER TEEN AGE 16+

AS SEEN ON CARTOON NETWORK!

MY-HiME

BY KIMURA NOBORU AND SATO KEN-ETSU

Two highly competitive, rival schoolgirls. One overzealous boy. And that's just the start of the trouble! When Fuuka Academy is attacked by strange creatures called Orphans, the school sets up a special female task force—called HiMEs.

ACTION | M MATURE AGES 18+

LIFE

BY KEIKO SUENOBU

It's about real teenagers...
It's about real high school...
It's about real life.
Ayumu seems like a normal girl, but her life is in a downward spiral. Seeking solace in her friends, Ayumu is looking for herself down the wrong path.

STRAWBERRY MARSHMALLOW

BY BARASUI

Follow the lives of Nobue Ito, her younger sister Chika, and her friends Miu and Matsuri as these cute girls try to solve problems and help each other out in the most adorable ways! They're a joyful treat in this slice-of-life delight!

PEPPERMINT

BY EUN-JIN SEO

What do you do when true love is beyond your reach? Hey is an average teenage girl who has a crush on the hot pop star EZ. But whenever she tries to work up the nerve to confess her feelings toward him, drama gets in the middle of things! It seems EZ may only ever think of her as a fan...

ROMANCE

T TEEN AGE 13+

RECAST

BY SEUNG-HUI KYE

Can one boy use his recast powers to save the world? JD is a young boy raised by his grandfather to be the last hope for a world in conflict—too bad nobody told JD! Will he learn to master the powers he's been entrusted with?

"HARRY POTTER MIGHT HAVE COMPETITION!" –IGN.COM

WHEN LOVE GETS YOU DOWN... GRAB ANOTHER DRINK!
Pixie POP
GOKKUN PUCHO
TOKYOPOP
Mayu is unlucky with love until she meets Pucho, the magical fairy of beverages. Now, whenever Mayu drinks something, she transforms accordingly! Milk makes her grow large, water makes her invisible, pork soup turns her into a cute little piglet. But what will help her win the man of her dreams?
From Ema Toyama, author of *Tenshi no Tamago*, comes a bubbly manga that's sure to tickle your tastebuds!
Pixie POP
GOKKUN PUCHO
1
EMA TOYAMA
ROMANCE
T
TEEN AGE 13+
Gokkun Pucho © Ema Toyama / KODANSHA LTD.